35 Things I Wish I Knew Before my First Pregnancy

First Time Mom's Guide to an Empowering Pregnancy, Birth and Postpartum

Amira Roux

Table of Contents

Trigger Warning

This book may contain sensitive information about misperceptions regarding what's healthy and what's not.

Introduction

Who doesn't want an empowering pregnancy, birth, and postpartum? We all do, but we don't always have the proper knowledge and guidance to get where we want to be. We have access to a lot of resources, but sometimes we need a push in real life—someone who has the patience to walk us through their own experience, someone who can relate to what we are going through. We need someone who understands our fears and can share strategies to ease our mental, physical, and emotional pain. The author of *35 Things I Wish I Knew Before my First Pregnancy* wants to be *your* someone. What do you say?

About Amira Roux

Amira is a dedicated mom, wife, engineer, and program manager who feels pregnancy is not as scary as most people think when one takes steps to learn and prepare. She didn't know much about labor when she tried to learn through the internet, but soon realized scrolling through pins and reading blogs was not enough for her to prepare for the journey that awaited her. So, she put in more effort.

Having a healthy baby was Amira's non-negotiable priority when she had her first pregnancy. She created checklists and plans to ensure she was as healthy as possible. She also wanted a vaginal birth, and together with her doula, they prepared for that special time in her life. She had someone, she found people who guided her through the process. Through this comprehensive book, Amira aims to do the same for you. She wants to share essential knowledge she gained with experience, research, and external support. This book guide covers information from conception, labor, and delivery to postpartum life.

"I basically did everything I could to ensure I gave the best to my baby in terms of health. While I'm all about natural ways of doing things, I don't want to judge anyone who does things differently because, in the end, we all want what we think is right for our children. I just want to share from the perspective of a mom who tried to make as many healthy choices as possible to give the best to her baby," says Amira.

Chapter 1:

Your First Trimester: Get the Basics Right!

Whether you have been trying for a bubbling mini you or it just happened unexpectedly, it's crucial that you get the basics right from the beginning to enjoy the beautiful journey ahead. It won't be all rosy, but as long as you put effort into establishing the right foundation, you are going on an adventure!

Signs You Are Pregnant

Implantation Bleeding

From the first week of your pregnancy to the fourth, all of the changes are still taking place on a cellular level. The fertilization of your egg results in the formation of a fluid-filled cell that will later develop into your unborn baby's body parts and organs. This fluid-filled cell, called a blastocyst, implants in the lining of your uterus around the fourth week following conception. The implantation can result in bleeding that looks similar to light menstrual flow. While this is not something that happens to every woman, if it happens, it will most likely take place close to the time when you anticipate having your period.

The color of your spotting may have a brown tinge to it, but sometimes it may be red or pink. The amount of bleeding that you may experience during implantation is often substantially smaller than that of your menstrual period. This kind of bleeding shouldn't be heavy enough to necessitate a tampon or sanitary pad, as it won't even be enough to turn into a flow. Pain is also less intense than what you might experience during a typical menstrual period. Some women experience cramping during the implantation phase, but it should not hurt enough to confine them to bed.

Missed Period

After a fluid-filled cell successfully implants, your body starts producing a hormone called human chorionic gonadotropin (hCG). The hormone instructs your ovaries not to release mature eggs on a monthly basis, thereby stopping your monthly menstrual flow. HCG also assists your body in continuing to carry your unborn baby to term. At this point, your unborn baby is called an embryo.

Although you may miss your period after you hit the 4-week mark of your pregnancy journey, missing a period is not a guaranteed sign of pregnancy. Therefore, you may need to confirm your pregnancy by taking a test, especially if your past periods have been very unpredictable.

Breast Changes

Another early sign of pregnancy during your first trimester is a change in your breast size and how they feel. You may start noticing these changes between the fourth and sixth week of your pregnancy. Again, breast changes during pregnancy do not manifest the same way for every woman. You could experience a tingling sensation as your breasts increase in size. Slight aching is also a normal symptom during this time. This increase in growth occurs because of changes in hormone levels. Around the eleventh week, your breasts will continue to expand in size as your areola gets bigger and darker. Once your changing body adjusts to the new hormones, breast soreness and that swollen feel are likely to subside, then you will be comfortable again.

Sore nipples? You can alleviate nipple pain by purchasing breast pads that are designed to fit into your bra and prevent friction. You can get some relief from breast soreness by investing in a maternity bra that is both comfortable and supportive. Get yourself a comfortable bra that is made from cotton and does not have any underwire support. You can also make your bra choices efficient by picking one that has adjustable clasps so that it can accommodate the growth that awaits you in the next few months.

Frequent Urination

When you're pregnant, your kidneys process a higher volume of fluid compared to when you are your usual self. This is due to your body's need to pump more blood so it can support your growing baby. The resultant increase in bladder volume causes you to make frequent bathroom visits for relief, but that is not all. You may also experience a lot of accidental leaks during normal activities.

Does that sound embarrassing? You can try scheduling your trips to the bathroom to avoid embarrassing leaks and unwelcome discomfort. You should also consume an additional fluid amount to avoid dehydration during pregnancy.

Appetite Changes

It is also possible for your sense of smell and taste to shift during the early phase of your pregnancy. Obviously, such changes would also interfere with your dietary choices because, who wants to eat food that smells like the end of the world? Okay, so no more onions and eggs, your stomach says. You may come up with an endless list of foods that no longer taste good and those you think smell weird. If you don't properly think about your diet while you are pregnant, you may end up eating way less than you should, and that would be bad for both you and your growing bundle of cuteness.

Nausea

You may also experience morning sickness between your fourth and sixth week of pregnancy. In most women, this sick feeling reaches its worst point in the ninth week. Morning sickness is not morning sickness, don't let the name deceive you! When you are pregnant, nausea can strike at any time of the day, and it certainly won't wait for the morning if it decides to visit you at night. The severity of morning sickness varies from woman to woman, but if you experience vomiting so severe you can't keep anything down, do not hesitate to call your healthcare provider. Remember to consume a lot of fluids to replace the water you lose when vomiting.

As you draw close to the end of your first trimester, you may also notice an increase in your weight.

Fetal Development

There are three primary stages that occur during the process of prenatal development. The first two weeks after you conceive are referred to as the germinal stage. After that comes the embryonic period, which occurs from the third week through the eighth. From the ninth week to the time your baby is ready to leave the womb. This is known as the fetal period (Cherry, 2020).

Germinal Phase

When your egg cell and a sperm cell join together in one of your fallopian tubes during conception, this marks the beginning of the germinal stage. During this time, your baby is called a zygote. The single-celled zygote makes its way down the fallopian tube and into your uterus a few hours following conception. Now, your baby is in the making! The process of cell division usually starts within an average of two days following conception. The zygote undergoes a process called mitosis in order to divide into two cells. After that, it divides into four cells, then eight cells, and so on.

If your baby made it past the first phase, that is worth a smile because a sizable percentage of zygotes do not advance past this early stage of cell division. When there are eight cells present, the cells start differentiating and adopting certain features that eventually decide the function of each cell. This process continues until there are twenty cells present. When the cells divide, they form two distinct masses: the cells on the outside will develop into the placenta, and those on the inside become part of the embryo.

During the zygote's journey to the uterine wall, the cell division rate never slows. Once there, the process of implantation is not a straightforward one, but if it is successful, your hormones disrupt the menstrual cycle, and you experience a wide variety of changes to your body. We have already discussed some of those changes, but the list of changes you may experience at this time goes on. Over the following months of your pregnancy, the connective network of blood vessels and membranes between your growing baby and your uterus supplies the nutrients needed for growth and survival.

Embryonic Phase

Your baby is now an embryo! The embryonic phase of development begins three weeks following conception. During this stage, the mass of cells begins to take on the characteristics of a human being. The major catch during this stage of embryonic development is the formation of the brain. Your growing baby's neural tube and the neural plate form around the fourth week following conception. The neural tube will grow your baby's central nervous system at some point in the future. One of the earliest indicators that your baby's neural tube is developing well is the appearance of two ridges on the neural plate.

Over the course of the next few days, additional ridges will grow and fold inward, eventually producing a hollow tube. When this tube has completely developed, cells will start to form around its center. The neural tube starts to seal off, and vesicles begin to develop in the brain. The brain vesicles will eventually grow into various sections of the brain.

In the fourth week of development, your baby's head starts to shape. Shortly after the head forms, facial organs such as the nose, mouth, and eyes emerge. The blood vessel that will form your baby's heart also gets to work and starts beating. During your little one's fifth week of development, the buds that eventually become their legs and arms appear. At the end of the eighth week of your little one's development, they have developed all of the fundamental organs and parts, with the exception of their sex organs. At this stage, the embryo is only a gram in weight and approximately an inch in length.

By the time the embryonic phase comes to an end, the fundamental features of your baby's brain are set up. The synthesis of neurons, also known as brain cells, begins approximately 42 days after conception and continues throughout the majority of the pregnancy, culminating some time close to the middle of your third trimester (Stiles and Jernigan, 2010). As neurons develop, they move to their final destinations throughout the brain. As soon as they arrive at their positions, they start forming connections with other brain cells, ultimately establishing fundamental neural networks.

Fetal Phase

Your growing baby is now a fetus! Your baby becomes a fetus after the majority of the cells in the embryo have differentiated into their respective types, and the embryo advances to the subsequent stage. This stage of development starts around the ninth week of pregnancy and continues right up to birth. This period is characterized by extraordinary development and change. During this stage of prenatal development, also known as fetal development, more significant changes occur in your baby's brain. The structures and systems of your baby's body that developed during the embryonic period continue to grow more defined.

As neurons continue to grow, your baby's spinal cord and brain emerge from the neural tube and *synapses*, the links between neurons, start to develop. Between Week 9 and 12, reflexes start developing, and the fetus can make involuntary movements with its legs and arms. When the fetus is in its third month of development, its sexual organs begin to distinguish from one another. All of your baby's body parts fully mature into defined human forms by the end of the third month. Around this time, the fetus reaches a weight of about three ounces. Although most of your baby's physical growth takes place in later phases of the pregnancy, they continue to increase in length as well as weight after organ differentiation. Your first trimester ends at the end of your third month of pregnancy.

Changing Emotions

It is normal to experience a range of feelings regarding your pregnancy, regardless of whether or not you intended to become pregnant. It is okay if you go from being very excited about that second line to being highly uncertain about what lies ahead. You can go from happy to sad and back to happy within a space of minutes; that is normal. If you hadn't planned to become a new mom, you may even blame your partner or feel very bad about it. During your first trimester, hormones such as progesterone and estrogen play a role in stirring up a roller coaster of feelings in your body.

Because of the hormonal shifts taking place in you, you may experience intensified feelings, both pleasant and negative. You could be absolutely delighted about having a kid, but at the same time, you might also feel pressured, burdened, and unready. It is also possible that you may experience a lot of anxiety in relation to your pregnancy and the prospect of becoming a new parent. You might also feel unhappy about the changes in your body. This can stir up concerns about losing or gaining too much weight. We all worry about the possibility of not fitting into our favorite dresses at some point. Maybe that is the womanly thing to do. Pregnancy can also cause you to worry about being unable to participate in some of the physical activities you are accustomed to. And, well, which woman doesn't want to impress their partner? During your first trimester, you may also worry about appearing unattractive to your loved one.

When you combine these mixed emotions and endless worries that your pregnancy hormones may cause, you may feel as though your life is about to slip through your fingers. But no, you are still very much in control! All you have to do is take care of yourself.

Many expecting women have an understandable worry, but in unfortunate instances, a few develop depression or anxiety disorders requiring medical intervention. Many of these women may not seek assistance to avoid embarrassment. However, anxiety disorders and depression require proper management that you will miss out on if you try to hide the problem. Getting the appropriate treatment for mental problems during your pregnancy is essential because, if left untreated, they can impact your ability to go on and affect even the welfare of your baby.

Cravings

With all the food cravings and aversions taking place during the first trimester of pregnancy, I had to be sure what to eat and what not to so I took a course about eating healthy. You can experience pregnancy cravings at any time—when you are preparing to leave for work in the morning or when you have just finished making a different dish for dinner. Food cravings during pregnancy come on so strong you would go to any lengths to satisfy your hunger for something even when you cannot find it close by.

In spite of the fact that some of your pregnancy cravings can be rather fulfilling and entertaining, you still have to make an effort to maintain some level of restraint. That is because giving in to all the cravings you have during pregnancy is not always the greatest choice for your baby's health. Try some of the following ways to deal with your pregnancy cravings.

- Opt for healthy snacks
    - You are more likely to start seeking random items when you are hungry, particularly things that are high in carbohydrates or sugar. If you keep some nutritious snacks on hand, you will be able to quickly munch your cravings away whenever the feeling of hunger strikes. To prepare for whatever taste your cravings sway you toward, you should be sure to prepare both sweet and savory snacks. It's a brilliant idea to carry nutritious snacks in your handbag whenever you are stepping out to avoid buying unhealthy snacks at the last minute. Consuming foods such as seeds and nuts, which have healthy fats, proteins, and carbohydrates, helps you feel satiated for a longer period of time. Fruit is another fantastic option for a healthy snack when you are pregnant. Bananas and apples are two examples of fruits that are easy to transport and consume anywhere you go. You can also stock up on nutritious cookies so that you can satisfy your sweet cravings

without consuming an excessive amount of added sugar.

- Break it down

    o Avoid serving yourself large portions of food when you are pregnant. This helps keep you from throwing up during and just after meals. Another benefit of splitting your servings is to avoid careless eating when you feel hungry. Consuming meals in small servings and a few bite-sized snacks on a daily basis is an excellent strategy for warding off cravings. Being well-prepared for pregnancy cravings by organizing your meals in advance will help you soar above unhealthy eating during pregnancy.

- Remember fluids

    o When you are dehydrated, you may have feelings of hunger, fatigue, nausea, and cloudy thinking. You have a larger water intake requirement and become dehydrated more quickly during pregnancy than before. It gets even worse if you often throw up during the early phase of your pregnancy. Increasing the amount of water you drink to ensure that you are well hydrated helps curb your desire to eat unhealthy foods. Try grabbing a glass of water and drinking it slowly whenever you feel your body telling you to eat more than you should or when you crave something unhealthy.

Prenatal Testing

When you are pregnant, you can undergo prenatal testing to assess whether or not your unborn child is at risk of inheriting any genetic disorders or being born with any birth defects. Taking prenatal tests to optimize the prognosis for your little human helps to determine different possibilities for your pregnancy or special care during the course of your adventure. Depending on what the woman is currently in and there are a few different prenatal tests you can take depending on the stage of your pregnancy and the nature of the condition being evaluated.

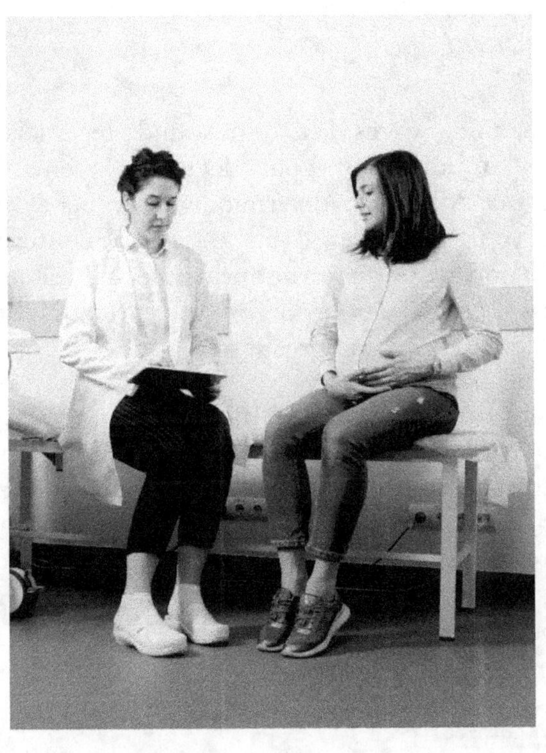

During your pregnancy, you can take two primary forms of prenatal testing. The first test screens your chances of giving birth to a baby who has birth defects. If you have a higher than average risk of having a baby with a certain chromosomal abnormality, you are identified through screening procedures. These screening tests are unable to detect birth problems such as hereditary disorders. If you test positive, you will have to undergo further testing. The tests used for screening are not the same as diagnostic tests. Diagnostic testing can establish whether or not your growing fetus is affected by a certain congenital condition or genetic disorder.

Ultrasound

Using sound waves, an ultrasound technician can produce an image of your developing fetus in the uterus. In addition to determining how far along you are in your pregnancy, this test also confirms the position and size of your unborn child, as well as looks for any potential anomalies in the structure of your unborn child's growing organs and bones.

In the 11th through the 14th week of pregnancy, you will go for a specialized ultrasound that is termed a nuchal translucency ultrasound. The ultrasound will check for a collection of fluid behind your baby's neck. If there is an abnormally large amount of fluid, this indicates that there is an increased risk of Down syndrome.

Blood Tests

Your healthcare provider may request two different forms of blood screening in the first trimester of your pregnancy. The tests, a serum integrated screening test, and a sequential integrated screening test, are ordered in the process of determining the concentrations of particular compounds in blood: human chorionic gonadotropin and a pregnancy-associated plasma protein-A. The presence of excessive amounts of either compound indicates an increased risk of chromosomal abnormalities.

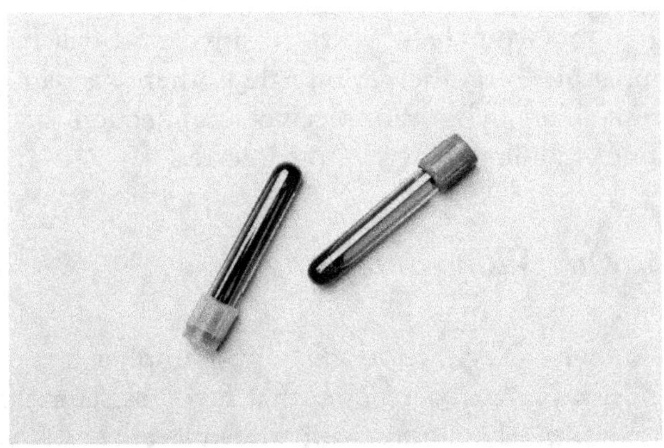

Your health care providers may check your blood to see whether or not you were protected against rubella. They may also screen you for syphilis, hepatitis B, HIV, and any signs of anemia at your first prenatal visit.

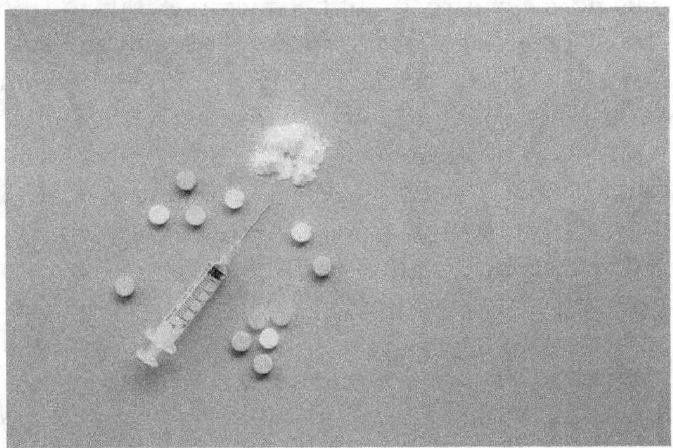

Depending on your genetic makeup, you are either rhesus-positive or rhesus negative. Although the majority of people have a positive rhesus (Rh) factor, if you are Rh-negative, your body will create antibodies that affect your future pregnancies. If you are Rh-negative, but your baby is Rh-positive, you will be Rh incompatible. In the event that there is an Rh incompatibility, you can receive an injection of Rh-immune globulin in your third trimester.

Chorionic Villus Sampling

Also known as CVS, chorionic villus sampling is a form of invasive prenatal screening that involves removing a tiny sample of tissue from the placenta. If your physician reviews the findings of an earlier noninvasive screening procedure and finds anything suspicious, they might recommend chorionic villus sampling for further investigations.

CVS is normally carried out between the 10th and 12th weeks of pregnancy. This procedure can show genetic disorders, such as cystic fibrosis, and chromosomal abnormalities, such as Down syndrome. CVS is in two different kinds: One form of CVS is called a transabdominal test, while the other kind is called a transcervical test. Both kinds of tests are performed by inserting a probe into the patient's abdomen or cervix. The testing can cause uncomfortable side effects such as spotting or cramping. CVS also carries a possibility of the pregnancy not continuing, but the good news is that it is a voluntary examination, and you are not required to complete it if you don't want to do so.

Chapter 2:

Your Second Trimester:

Dealing With Typical

Pregnancy Fears

Congratulations! You are now in the second trimester of your pregnancy. Time has flown, right? If you are not yet in the second trimester and you are still wandering, trying to find answers about what the second trimester of pregnancy feels like, then keep reading because this is an informative section about the second trimester. You can look forward to some desirable shifts when you reach this benchmark.

Signs You Should be Aware Of

To begin with, the majority of the early pregnancy symptoms you have will start to improve or even go away completely. This is good news. It means you can now eat food that you used to skip earlier in your pregnancy. Your taste and smell have been restored, and your energy levels should be picking up. Although your breasts are still more prominent, they should feel a lot less tender.

Before you go further, it is important to know that the second trimester of pregnancy runs from Week 13 and continues until the 28th week. Approximately fourteen weeks pass during the second trimester of your pregnancy. In the second trimester, symptoms such as nausea and vomiting (gravidarum emesis), body weakness, and breast tenderness that you used to experience, fade or become less serious than before. Others, such as heartburn and constipation, may continue for the remainder of the pregnancy.

During this same time, some developments may manifest themselves for the first time as your abdomen expands and the hormone production levels keep increasing in your body. These new hormonal changes will make you experience some of the following symptoms:

- dizziness
    - You might start experiencing dizziness if you have not already started. If you have already noticed signs of dizziness but are not taking iron supplements, it might turn out to be worse during this period. This is a result of your blood vessels widening and relaxing to increase the blood flow to your baby while decreasing your blood pressure and hemodilution, an increase in blood plasma levels as compared to your

blood cells. This, combined with the increased iron demand for both you and your growing baby, can lead to anemia. To alleviate dizziness, try to consume a large number of small food portions, drink plenty of fluids, take your daily iron supplements, and rest as much as possible.

- weight gain

  - You will see an increase in your body weight due to your fetus in the uterus growing and your uterus enlarging. Your amniotic fluid is also increasing, and your appetite is picking up. If you fell pregnanct at an average weight, expect to gain six to fourteen pounds during this trimester.

- lower abdominal pain

  - Also known as round ligament pain, lower abdominal pain is a common symptom of pregnancy that occurs when the ligaments that support your abdomen stretch to accommodate the growing size of your belly.

- nasal congestion

  - An increase in blood flow to the mucus membranes in your nose may cause you to experience nasal congestion, resulting in difficulty breathing. You might even start snoring in your sleep even if you have never snored a night in your life! If nasal congestion persists, see your doctor, as they may prescribe some over-the-counter medication that is safe for you and your unborn baby.

- quickening

  - Those friendly kicks you start to feel in your abdomen are called quickening. They are a good sign that your little one is moving in the uterus. Quickening happens around the sixteenth to the twentieth week.

- mild swelling of the ankles and feet

  - After the 20th week of pregnancy, you may experience mild swelling in your ankles and feet. Some women notice this swelling earlier, and it may continue until delivery. If you want to minimize the appearance of puffiness, you should try to maintain an active lifestyle, prop your feet up when you are not moving, and avoid prolonged periods of standing or sitting. It is also important to watch your blood pressure to rule out conditions that are associated with this symptom.

- leg cramps

  - These often begin in the second trimester and continue into the third. Apart from contributing factors such as weight gain and hormonal changes, a deficiency in calcium and magnesium may also cause you to experience leg cramps. To prevent this from happening, make sure to maintain a nutritious blacked diet while you are pregnant.

- sensitive gums

  - This is due to hormonal changes, which will lead to inflammation or plaque, which might lead to bleeding. Don't hesitate to contact your dentist if your gums bleed or you notice anything unusual.

Fetal Development

Your unborn child is beginning to look more human as your pregnancy continues. Your fetus, which was a collection of cells in the first trimester, now has working muscles, nerves, and organs.

Below is the estimated development of your fetus that you can use to better understand what's taking your beautiful baby so long to get in your arms.

Week 13: The baby's urine develops.

- Your baby starts producing pee at 13 weeks of gestation. The urine comes from some swallowed amniotic fluid then passes through the kidney for excretion. Your unborn baby's skeleton starts stiffening, especially the long bones and skull. Although it is still transparent and thin, your fetus will soon have thick skin.

Week 15: Your little one's scalp pattern changes.

- Your baby is growing quickly around 13 to 15 weeks into the pregnancy. Your fetus's bone is still growing and will soon show up on ultrasound scans. The hair pattern on your baby's scalp is also developing. Your unborn baby's eyes move in week 14. Your baby's head is upright after 16 weeks into your pregnancy. The synchronized limb motions of your baby can be seen during ultrasound exams. These motions, though, are still too minute for you to notice. Your baby should be weighing around four ounces and measures close to 4.75 inches in length.

Week 17: The baby's toenails grow in.

- Toenails start to grow 15 weeks after conception or 17 weeks into your pregnancy. In the amniotic sac, your baby is moving more and rolling and flipping. Each day, their heart pumps around 100 quarts of blood.

Week 18: Your unborn baby starts to hear.

- Your baby's ears start protruding from the sides of their head at about 18 weeks of pregnancy. Their eyes are starting to turn toward the front.

They can hear you talk and sing, but their all-time music is the sound from your digestive system. The digestive system of your newborn has begun to function. In the 18th week, your little one should measure about 6.75 inches in length.

Week 19: Your unborn grows a protective layer.

- Growth slows down at 19 weeks of pregnancy. Your baby starts to develop vernix caseosa, a greasy, cheese-like covering. The vernix caseosa aids in guarding against the abrasions, chapping, and hardening that can happen when your baby's skin gets in contact with amniotic fluid.

Week 20: You have reached the midpoint!

- You may begin to feel your baby's movements at 18 weeks following conception or halfway through your pregnancy. That is the quickening we discussed earlier. Your unborn baby wakes and sleeps at regular intervals. Your movements or noises will awaken the little one. You can also see the sex of your growing fetus via ultrasound.

Week 21: Your little one can suck their thumb.

- This is your baby developing a sucking reflex, and their entire body is covered with lanugo, a fine, downy hair. The lanugo holds the vernix caseosa firmly against your little one's skin.

Week 22: The unborn baby's hair starts to grow in.

- Your baby's eyebrows and hair are evident during 22 weeks of pregnancy. Additionally, brown fat is developing, which is where heat is produced. If your baby is a boy, his testicles have started to descend.

Week 23: Your baby's footprints and fingerprints develop.

- Your baby starts moving their eyes quickly during 23 weeks of pregnancy. Their palms and soles also develop ridges, which subsequently serve as the basis for fingerprints and imprints. You may feel jerking movements when the developing *mini you* have hiccups.

Week 24: Your baby has wrinkles!

- Your baby's skin is wrinkled, translucent, and pink due to visible blood in the capillaries.

Week 25: Baby responds to your voice

- By Week 25 or 23 weeks after conception, your baby may be able to move in response to familiar sounds, like your favorite song and voice.

Week 26: The baby's lungs grow.

- Your baby's lungs start producing surfactant, the chemical that helps the air sacs in the lungs to expand and prevents them from collapsing and sticking together when they deflate.

Week 27: Your baby continues to grow as the third trimester draws close.

- You've got this! Your little one is gaining weight, so their skin appears smoother. Their neurological system is still developing by the end of the second trimester.

Common Pregnancy Fears

- squashing the baby
    - You might worry that if you sleep on your abdomen, you could accidentally trample on your unborn child. It's comforting to know that your body will protect the baby on its own. It will become exceedingly challenging to roll over if you are used to sleeping on your abdomen plus, if anything, you are most likely to feel the pain before it gets to your unborn bundle.

- miscarriage
    - Although many miscarriages occur in the first trimester, when many women are often unaware that they are pregnant, you may still find yourself worried about its probability in the

second trimester. Miscarriages often result due to a chromosomal defect that prevents the fetus from developing normally, but the risk of miscarriage declines after the first trimester. When you stay cautious and give up unhealthy habits such as smoking and drinking alcohol, you can reduce your risk of this occurrence.

- poor nutrition due to morning sickness

  - Morning sickness won't lead to any nutritional imbalances or negative effects on the fetus unless you are so sick that you get dangerously dehydrated and you can't keep anything down. If that becomes the case, you should call or visit your doctor. Just remember to take your prenatal vitamins and eat small portions often. Eating like that makes things easier on your digestive system. The food that goes to your little bundle contains all the nutrition they need.

- harmful foods and other substances

  - It is only natural to overthink every time you analyze food labels or receive exotic food because we often receive tons of advice on what to eat and what to avoid. It is crucial to realize that all of the advice we get, is given with extreme caution, but even if you accidentally consume a small amount of the

unrecommended foods, you often don't
have to panic.

- early labor

  - This risk exists, particularly if you
    smoke or have an illness. You are more
    likely to undergo preterm labor if you
    are carrying twins or more, or if you
    have a previous history of early labor.
    The advancements in the healthcare
    system provide methods that can assist
    to prolong pregnancy, so preterm labor
    does not necessarily result in premature
    birth. However, you should contact
    your doctor if you have any such
    concerns.

- birth defects

  - Ensure you take prenatal vitamins daily
    to lower the chance of brain and spinal
    problems. Religiously taking prenatal
    supplements is an excellent approach to
    protect your unborn child. You should
    also take a multivitamin containing folic
    acid before becoming pregnant. If you
    didn't, you can still take them once you
    find out you are pregnant. Remember to
    discuss any specific worries you may
    have with your doctor. Your doctor
    should be able to offer you a clear
    understanding of the possible dangers
    and assist you in putting your worries
    into perspective when you provide them
    with your family history and age.

- medical complications such as pre-eclampsia

  - Not every pregnant woman experience *pre-eclampsia*, a condition that dangerously raises blood pressure in pregnant women. It is more likely to occur in women under the age of 18 and those over the age of 35. If you have any risk factors such as previous or family history of the condition, or a pre-existing blood pressure problem, your doctor will constantly monitor and advise you as the pregnancy progresses.

  - Note that pre-eclampsia sometimes doesn't appear until the second half of pregnancy. Prenatal and routine antenatal blood pressure monitoring will assist your medical team to detect the condition on time, should it occur. While we currently don't have methods to minimize the risk of pre-eclampsia, an early diagnosis can help control it. Report any preeclampsia symptoms, such as swelling in your feet, headaches, or blurred vision to your doctor.

  - The risks are also minimal for *gestational diabetes*, a condition in which your body is unable to digest sugar effectively, causing glucose to build up in the bloodstream. Bringing gestational diabetes under control normally requires minor dietary adjustments, such as reducing your intake of starchy carbohydrates. Between weeks 24 and

28 of pregnancy, a routine blood glucose test can detect diabetes in healthy women without a history of the disease.

Pregnancy Nutrition

A healthy pregnancy diet is crucial for both you and your unborn child because your food and liquid intake throughout pregnancy serves as the baby's primary source of nutrition. To offer the vital nutrients a baby needs for growth and development, as an expecting mother, it is advised that you eat a range of healthful foods and beverages. Here are some recommendations for a healthy pregnancy diet, including what foods to consume and avoid while pregnant and the reasons behind those decisions.

Foods to Eat

Vegetables and fruits

You can eat vegetables and fruits such as:

red peppers

- spinach

- cooked greens

- potatoes

- carrots

- grapefruit

- kiwi fruit

- watermelon

- peaches

- raspberries

- bananas

- pears

Fruits and vegetables make up a large portion of a healthy pregnancy diet because they are low in calories and high in fiber, vitamins, and minerals.

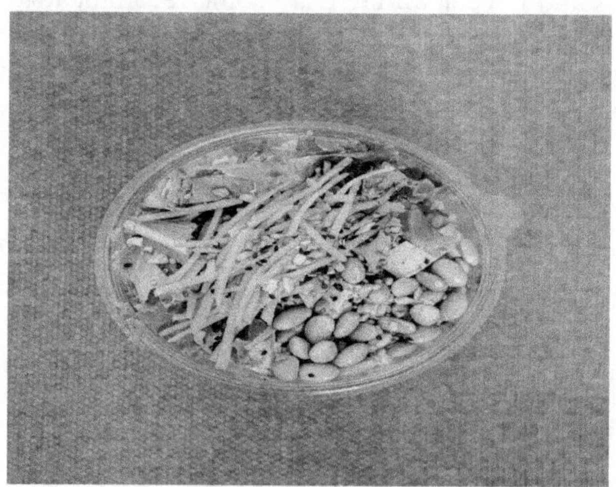

Some dairy products

Consume some dairy, preferably low-fat or fat-free yogurt, skim or 1% milk, and soymilk for calcium and vitamin D. Calcium is crucial for the construction of your little human's bones and teeth. If you don't get enough calcium, your body will get it from your bone reserves and send it to the baby to satisfy the increasing pregnancy needs.

Proteins

You find protein in fish, beef, beans, peas, nuts, and seeds. Protein aids in the development of your baby's vital organs, including the brain and heart. During pregnancy, you require at least 60 grams of protein daily.

Foods to Avoid

Raw meat and undercooked food

Stay away from raw undercooked food as it may contain parasites or bacteria that are harmful to you and the baby. *Listeriosis*, an infection brought on by the Listeria bacterium, is a serious health risk during pregnancy. The same goes for *toxoplasmosis*, an infection brought on by Toxoplasma gondii parasites. These infections have the potential to result in miscarriage, stillbirth, preterm labor, infant sickness, or even death.

- unwashed fruits and vegetables
  - Always properly wash raw fruits and vegetables to get rid of any harmful microorganisms. Steer clear of raw sprouts of any kind and ensure you adequately cook them when you *do* eat sprouts.

- fish with increased mercury levels
  - Certain varieties of fish like tuna, tilefish, shark, marlin, and swordfish have high levels of methylmercury and should be avoided while pregnant. Regular consumption of high-mercury seafood can cause mercury to build up in the bloodstream, which, when consumed, can harm your unborn child's developing brain and neurological system.

- alcohol

o When pregnant, stay away from alcohol. Through the umbilical cord, alcohol in your blood can immediately reach the unborn child. Fetal alcohol spectrum disorders, a range of illnesses that can cause physical issues as well as learning and behavioral issues in babies, have been related to heavy alcohol use during pregnancy.

- caffeine.

    o Although caffeine can pass the placenta, it is unclear how it will affect your unborn child. To be safe, your doctor may advise avoiding caffeine during pregnancy or limiting your intake to less than 200 milligrams (mg) per day.

    o Regardless of whatever you eat during pregnancy, remember to consume a lot of fluids. You can get enough fluids by consuming several glasses of water every day.

Food Handling

When handling and cooking food, abide by these general food safety recommendations:

- Wash your food before cooking.

    o Prior to consumption, slicing, or cooking, thoroughly rinse all raw vegetables under running water from the faucet.

- Clean up after yourself.

    o Once you have handled and prepared uncooked items, wash your hands, utensils, surfaces, and cutting boards.

- Thoroughly cook your food before eating.

    o Thoroughly cook your meat and ensure that your food is well-cooked to kill all microbes.

- Use proper food storage measures.

    o Cover and refrigerate all perishable goods when you are not using them.

Preparing for Amniocentesis

During an amniocentesis procedure, your healthcare provider removes a tiny amount of *amniotic fluid* from the amniotic sac for examination purposes. Amniotic fluid is the liquid that surrounds the fetus to protect it from injury and infection. It contributes to fetal development and allows your little one to *swim* around in the womb.

Amniotic fluid contains proteins, enzymes, and hormones, just to mention a few substances. It also has genetic information used to diagnose any genetic abnormalities in your unborn bundle. Based on your family history, your healthcare team may conduct tests to look for metabolic abnormalities and inherited gene problems; these issues include Patau syndrome, Down syndrome, and Edward syndrome. The same also applies if you have a family history of blood disorders such as thalassemia and sickle cell.

Amniocentesis is performed during the second trimester, around the 20th week of your pregnancy. It is totally up to you if you don't want to have the procedure. If you do, you will need to give consent beforehand.

Because it is an invasive procedure, the risks of amniocentesis include miscarriage but again, it does not happen with every case. Other dangers include infection, bleeding from the needle puncture, and preterm labor. The chances of these happening are very low, but they are possible risks. If you want to learn further about the risks involved, your doctor will advise you as necessary.

What to Expect

Typically, there is no need for additional preparation before an amniocentesis. You can prepare by eating and drinking as usual. Your doctor will let you know if you should have a full bladder before your visit. When taking the test, you can bring someone along with you for moral support.

Before and after the amniocentesis, you will undergo an ultrasound scan to determine your little one's position, if the needle can safely pass through the uterus and abdominal walls, and the ideal location to extract the amniotic fluid. You could receive anesthesia through your abdomen before your healthcare provider puts the needle there. They will first clean your abdomen with an antiseptic solution to reduce the possibility of infection, then puncture your abdominal wall using a long, thin needle. You may feel a strong stinging feeling after the insertion. Your doctor navigates into the amniotic sac using the ultrasound image as a guide, then uses a syringe to draw a little amniotic fluid for analysis.

Although amniocentesis seldom hurts, you could experience some discomfort while having it done. It's typical to experience cramps that resemble period pain and minor vaginal bleeding, for a few hours following amniocentesis. If you feel any discomfort, you can use over-the-counter medications like paracetamol. Please take note that you cannot just take any painkillers during pregnancy. If you are in doubt or need more information, your doctor will advise on which one is safe.

Checking Gender

If you have made the decision to learn your baby's sex while you are pregnant, you probably can't wait to hear it. Nowadays, many approaches make it possible for you to learn your baby's sex earlier compared to waiting for childbirth.

The sex of your baby is determined by chromosomal complement. Normally a person has 46 chromosomes. Two X chromosomes (46XX) are the chromosomes present in females, while one X and one Y chromosome are present in males (46 XY). The sperm will either contribute an X or Y chromosome since an egg only has one X chromosome. Therefore, The father is the one who decides the gender of the child, yes, not you.

Before we look at how you can find the gender of your baby, let's briefly look at the pros and cons of knowing your baby's gender.

Cons

No room for surprises. Some parents or new parents feel it's more enjoyable to wait until the baby is born than to find out in advance. If you are one of those that love to be surprised, knowing the gender before its time can take away the joy that comes with the element of surprise

Disappointment: if you were hoping for a girl, but you learn ahead of time that you're most likely expecting a male, this can make you feel less excited and anticipatory for the delivery.

Pros

- saves naming time
  - You won't list down both girl and boy names and start second guessing which

name you will pick because you already know the gender of your baby.

- adequate preparation

  - When you know the gender of your child, you might prepare the closet and pick out the colors you think are suitable for your baby. Additionally, you might enjoy hosting a gender reveal party and receiving more unique baby shower presents.

- more profound connection

  - Learning your baby's gender during pregnancy might make you feel more connected to your child, and the baby will become more of a reality.

Ultrasound

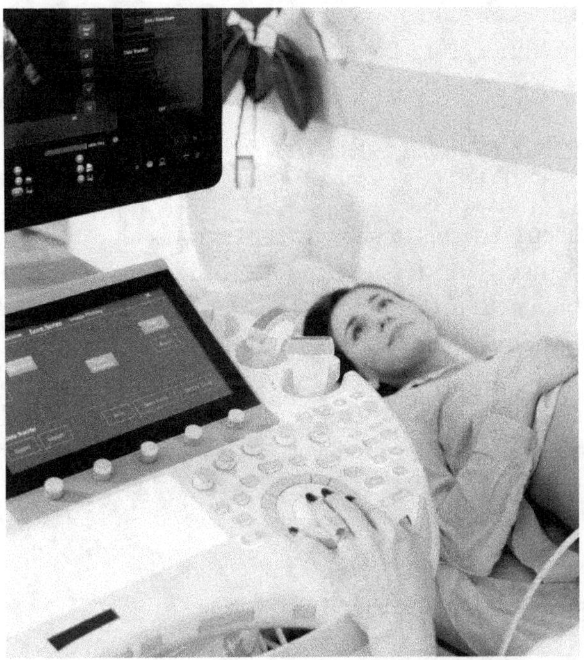

A baby's external genitalia is entirely developed by around 14 weeks of gestation. Thus, an ultrasound performed at any point after that might assist in identifying the gender of the child. However, 18 to 20 weeks is the best time to do it because the anatomy will have fully developed by then.

Non-Invasive Prenatal Testing

NIPT, also known as cell-free DNA testing, is a blood test designed to look for chromosomal abnormalities and conditions in a baby. The test examines a sample of your blood to check for minute pieces of fetal DNA that have been discharged into your circulation from the placenta while its main goal is to analyze fetal abnormalities, NIPT can also detect your baby's sex.

Chorionic Villus Sampling (CVS)

We discussed this test in the previous chapter. CVS is mainly used for testing genetic abnormalities and can also be used in detecting the gender of your unborn bundle. This method is used to access the placenta and collect a tiny sample of placental tissue for testing. Similar to NIPT, CVS tests placental cells to check for genetic anomalies, but it can also determine the sex of the baby.

Tips to Sleep Well

After a long day battling with your craving, work, and carrying your unborn bundle, you want to rest. Your body restores and fixes itself when you sleep. It's how your blood vessels heal, which is crucial considering how much strain your blood vessels are now under from the additional blood flow needed to sustain your growing unborn. Finding that position in which you used to feel comfortable in before you were pregnant is now difficult.

While sleeping on your right side is also appropriate when you're pregnant, It is usually advised to sleep on your left side. For apparent reasons, it becomes hard to rest on your abdomen after the first trimester. As an expecting mother, you shouldn't stress too much about your sleeping posture and should instead choose whatever is most comfortable for you.

You should refrain from sleeping on your back during the second and third trimesters. Why? The major vein that returns blood from your lower body to your heart, your vena cava, and your intestines all bear the full weight of your developing uterus and baby while you lie on your back. This pressure may exacerbate backaches, impair circulation, reduce digestion, and perhaps result in low blood pressure, which can induce lightheadedness.

Add as many comfortable pillows as you like to get a good night's sleep during this time. If you have trouble falling asleep, try crossing one leg over the other and placing a cushion between your legs and another behind your back.

There are other simple tricks you can use to control sleep disruptions when you are pregnant. Create the mood, don't just flop onto your bed. A pleasant, quiet, dark setting and a reasonable temperature promotes better sleep. You can also enhance your quality of sleep by going to bed and waking up around the same time every day. Practice switching off electronics before heading to bed.

Sex During Pregnancy

You probably have a lot of questions concerning the topic at hand, and the first one is probably whether you should abstain during pregnancy. Is it safe to have sex while you are pregnant? Will your unborn be hurt? What are the best positions?

Except if your doctor has warned against it, having sex while pregnant is totally safe. Your uterus cannot be penetrated by a penis or other penetrative sex object. The amniotic fluid in your womb and the uterus's tough muscles both provide protection for your unborn. As long as you don't have difficulties like premature labor or placenta abnormalities, having sexual activity won't harm your unborn child. It is important to know that sexual activity won't cause a miscarriage during pregnancy. The reason for the majority of miscarriages is an abnormally growing fetus.

How will your pregnancy affect libido? You will start experiencing changes in your sexual desires during pregnancy. Nonetheless, this is common. Your libido might increase or totally decrease. Despite the fact that this is nothing to be concerned about, discussing it with your spouse might be beneficial.

Several sexual positions are acceptable during pregnancy as long as they make you feel comfortable. Having sex with your spouse on top might become unpleasant due to your growing belly and body aches you might experience. It could be preferable to lie on your sides with your spouse behind you or facing each other when doing it. You could also want to experiment with being on top while having sex or getting penetrated from behind while kneeling. Whatever works for you as long as you are comfortable

Are you wondering when you should avoid having sex during pregnancy? As mentioned before, your doctor will communicate with you in advance if they worry about any possible risks. Your doctor could advise against having sex if:

- the placenta is lying low, meaning it is partially or entirely covering your cervix

- you have an amniotic fluid leak

- you experience cervical insufficiency, a condition where your cervix opens up too soon in the second trimester

- you have a history of premature labor or premature rupture of membranes

- you notice vaginal bleeding

Chapter 3:

Your Third Trimester

Congratulations! Your Baby

Is on the Way

It's your 28th week and your third trimester. What a journey this has been! You are now looking forward to seeing what will happen as you enter your last 12 weeks of pregnancy. The third trimester runs from the 28th week to the 40th week. Your little one is on the way home, and you have a lot to prepare. This is the chapter to guide you through it and get you ready. Without wasting much time, let's walk through it.

Third Trimester Signs

- backaches

    - The hormones produced during pregnancy relax the ligaments that normally maintain your bones in place, particularly in the pelvic region. During the third trimester of pregnancy, these changes can be harsh on your back and can lead to uneasiness. When you sit, go for seats that provide adequate support for your back. Put on shoes with strong ankle support that have a low heel. Get in touch with your primary care physician if the pain is intense or continues for an extended period.

- spider veins

    - An increase in blood circulation may cause you to have reddish-purple veins, often known as spider veins, on your face, neck, and arms. They normally disappear after childbirth, restoring your bright, radiant appearance.

- varicose veins (hemorrhoids)

    - There is also a possibility that you will see bulging veins, often known as varicose veins, on your legs. Varicose veins in the rectal region, generally known as hemorrhoids, may also become painful and uncomfortable. To reduce swelling, try engaging in physical activity, elevating your legs often, consuming a diet high in fiber, and drinking a lot of water. Sitting in a warm tub or using witch hazel pads on the affected region might provide relief from hemorrhoids. Contact your physician if you have concerns or if the pain persists.

- frequent urination

    o As you reach the latter weeks of your pregnancy, you may discover that you feel like urinating more frequently than you used to. This is due to the fact that when your developing baby grows further down, into your pelvis, they exert pressure on your bladder. You could also discover that you have some bladder leakage, mainly when you laugh, cough, carry something heavy, or sneeze.

- fatigue

    o Because of the pressure that your pregnancy is placing on your body throughout this trimester, you should eat regularly and adequately, be active, and try not to compromise the quality of your sleep.

- acid indigestion (acid reflux)

    o Your growing baby is making your uterus grow bigger, which will eventually push your stomach acid upward in your esophagus, which will result in a burning sensation. Additionally, the hormones produced loosen up your sphincter muscles, making it easy for acid stomach content to regurgitate. The regurgitation will cause you to experience a burning feeling in your chest. Talk to your obstetrician about using antacids to know which ones are safe in your situation.

- frequent bowel movements

  - Because some of the muscle sphincters in your body relax as your body prepares for labor and delivery, you may have pre-labor diarrhea. Other contributing factors include changes in your diet, medication, and stress. If your symptoms prolong or you feel weak and dehydrated, you should make an appointment with your primary care provider.

- pain in the pelvic and abdominal region

  - You may experience cramping or significant discomfort around your tummy or pelvic region. The pain is due to your round ligaments, which support your lower abdominal region, stretch to accommodate your expanding baby bump.

- sleep problems

- During the third trimester, expect more trouble sleeping and waking up more frequently at night. The majority of pregnant women experience 4 to 5 episodes of sleep disturbance throughout the night, typically brought on by various discomforts such as the urge to pee, cramps, indigestion, and sometimes the movement of the fetus.

- weird dreams

  - It is common to experience nightmares and weird dreams in your third trimester. Even if the strangeness of your dreams continues to increase, that shouldn't let you stress over it. It is absolutely not out of the ordinary. Your dreams are only a reflection of your thoughts and fears about the impending arrival of your baby, so you have nothing to worry about.

- dry and itchy skin

  - You may notice itching when your skin expands and dries out due to the growth of your belly. It is relieving to drink water and gently massage the itching area with a moisturizing ointment.

- sore gums

  - When you clean or floss your teeth, your gums may feel sensitive, and they may swell or bleed. Rinsing your mouth

with salt water and using a brush with a
softer bristle provides relief.

- anxiety

  - When the reality of becoming a parent
    starts setting in, you may feel nervous,
    but the fear is nothing to lose sleep
    over. Try keeping a record of your ideas
    to help you remain composed.

- Braxton Hicks contractions

  - You will experience mild, irregular
    contractions in your abdomen at
    different times. They might happen
    after engaging in strenuous exercise or
    having a sexual encounter. As your due
    date gets closer, you will notice regular
    contractions, that get stronger with
    time. If your contractions become
    regular and strong, alert your doctor or
    let your caregivers know.

Third Trimester Baby Development

Week 28: CNS development and baby's eyes partly opening

- Your baby's eyes can open partially, and
  eyelashes have grown at 28 weeks of pregnancy.
  The ability of the central nervous system to
  regulate body temperature and regular breathing

motions has improved. While your unborn bundle is now able to survive outside the womb because their lungs can breathe air, they would require medical assistance. Your tiny human can now blink, suck thumbs, and cry. They should be around 14.5 inches and 2.6 pounds in size, and their hair might be covering their full head by now.

Week 29: Baby stretches and kicks

- Your baby may kick, stretch, and make grasping motions during week 29 of pregnancy. They should measure around 15.5 inches from head to heel and weigh about three pounds.

Week 30: Blood cells and baby's hair grow

- Your baby's eyes can open widely at 30 weeks of pregnancy. The bone marrow of your unborn bundle now produces red blood cells. Your baby practices breathing even though their lungs are still developing. The fetus can now absorb important minerals from the digestive system, including calcium and iron. From head to heel, your little one measures around 16 inches and weighs about 3.45 pounds.

Week 31: Baby starts gaining weight quickly

The mini you has finished most of their primary development at 31 weeks of gestation and it's now time to put on weight. Your baby is developing more plumpness and smoothness. The unborn baby can now urinate; thus, the amniotic fluid surrounding them is rising. They measure 16.6 inches in length and weigh around 3.9 pounds. Encourage your partner, friends and any relatives to speak to your growing baby so that they may form a strong bond with your baby when they begin to recognize sounds outside the womb.

Week 32: Skin changes

- The toenails on your unborn baby are now visible at 32 weeks. This week, the *lanugo*, a coat of soft hair covering baby's skin for the previous few months, begins to shed. Their skin is smooth and pink. The length of your unborn child is around 17 inches and they weigh about 4.3 pounds.

Week 33: Baby starts detecting light, bones begin to stiffen, lung maturation

- Your baby's pupils can enlarge in reaction to a stimulation brought on by light at week 33 of pregnancy. Their skull is still soft and malleable, and having a slightly flexible head facilitates easier passage through the birth canal. At this point, your fetus measures around 17.4 inches in length and weighs about 4.8 pounds.

Week 34: Fingernails and movement changes

- Your baby's fingernails have reached the tips of their fingers at 34 weeks gestation. Your growing baby is chubbier and rounder. It will get more difficult for the baby to move around as he grows. He may, however, twist, rotate, and stretch. Their testicles descend from the abdomen into the scrotum if you have a little boy inside. Your little one can now breathe on their own. Your fetus measures around 17.8 inches in length and weighs about 5.2 pounds.

Week 35: Your baby's skin is silky

- Your pregnancy is 35 weeks old, and your developing baby's skin is starting to smoothen. Their limbs look to be fat. Your baby measures around 18.3 inches in length and weighs 5.7 pounds.

Week 36: The baby occupies the majority of your uterus

- At 36 weeks into your pregnancy, the packed environment within your uterus may make it more difficult for your baby to kick freely. The baby may turn around in preparation to join the rest of the family. They also have a strong grip by this time. Your little one measures around 18.6 inches in length and weighs about 6.2 pounds.

Week 37: Your baby is now at early term

Even though they are now mature and ready for the world, your baby's brain and lungs are still developing. You might experience sporadic contractions and increased vaginal discharge. The labor process might start at any time.

Week 38: The baby keeps expanding

- The size of your baby's head and belly are roughly the same at 38 weeks of your pregnancy. Almost all of your baby's lanugo has fallen off. Your fetus measures around 19.4 inches in length and weighs a little over 7 pounds.

Week 39: The infant's chest is noticeable

- You are now full term. Your baby's chest is starting to show more. They have gained fat throughout their body to keep your baby warm after delivery. From head to heel, your fetus measures around 19.7 inches in length and weighs about 7.5 pounds.

Week 40: Hello baby!

- After 40 weeks of pregnancy, your fetus is now about 20 inches in length and 8 pounds in weight. You may have gotten used to bonding with them by massaging your belly, now they are ready to meet you in person!

If your due date passes without any symptoms of labor, don't panic. Get in touch with your doctor for further instructions. Bear in mind that different babies grow at their own paces so the length and weight may differ.

Tips on Prenatal Bonding

There is no rule that says you have to wait until your child is born to start bonding with them. During your pregnancy, you may find that you are in the ideal position to begin developing an attachment with your unborn child, which will be critical to your baby's growth after birth.

Your unborn's senses will continue to mature as they grow. The sensation of touch is the first sense that fully develops in humans. Eight weeks after conception, the baby's face will develop its first touch receptors. During your pregnancy, your body will produce more touch receptors in various locations.

At approximately 18 weeks, your baby's hearing begins to develop. At first, your unborn baby will be able to hear your voice and bowel sounds. Between the weeks of 27 and 29, they will be able to hear sounds that originate from the environment outside your body. Babies may remember certain pieces of music they heard while they were still in the womb. They will develop their sense of smell, taste, and sight before they are born, so there are various ways to stimulate them when bonding.

Bonding With the Baby

Here are practical ways to bond with your unborn and help you feel closer:

Massage your pregnant belly.

- Massaging your abdomen may give your little one a good sensation. Applying lotion to your skin in circular motions can help maintain suppleness and hydration. Your baby can benefit from having their mother massage the abdomen. Your unborn will be most alert and responsive when engaged in activities that include touch.

Serenade your unborn child.

- Whether you are a singer or not, it is a time-honored custom to express your affection through songs. When you start singing to your unborn baby, you will sense a stronger connection with them. During the final trimester of your pregnancy, your baby will pay close attention to the sound of your voice. You don't need to stress about what to sing because even the good old lullabies will do the trick.

Play familiar sounds.

- Listen to music together as a family. Lullabies and other types of music that simulate a heartbeat of around sixty beats per minute might be helpful for both you and your unborn baby. You may also do a search on the internet for music that is soothing or tranquil.

Preserve your sonography picture of your growing baby.

- A photo of your unborn child obtained from an ultrasound close at hand might make your pregnancy seem more genuine. It will become more of a reality that you have a newborn inside you growing, waiting to see the world.

Talk about your pregnancy and unborn baby with those close to you.

- Give other people the chance to feel your growing abdomen if you are comfortable with that. Make sure to inform the grandparents about your baby's developing movements. Ask about what your mother or mother-in-law used to do when they were pregnant.

You can write a letter to your baby.

- It is possible that thinking about your baby and increasing the amount of prenatal bonding you do by writing letters to your baby will be beneficial in a way that you will be able to hold talks in which you express the goals and aspirations you have for your life together. Additionally, you can make a pregnancy journal which you can give your child when they are adults.

Be attentive to your baby's kicks.

- Pay attention to the kicks your baby is giving you. When you are in your third and final trimester of pregnancy, you can try gently prodding the baby or rubbing your abdomen in the area where you felt the kick to see if there will be a reaction. This will allow you to feel closer and bond with your unborn, and you will have the realization that they truly are your very own tiny human being.

Read a book to the growing baby.

- Think about picking out some of your all-time favorite books for kids and starting the habit of reading to your unborn baby. You may start doing this as soon as you find out you are pregnant, but the benefits will be at their maximum in the second trimester of your pregnancy. Bonding with your unborn before delivery is not only a fantastic concept for you as a mom but also for fathers and other people in your immediate environment.

Prenatal Bonding for Your Partner

Your partner can gently rub your abdomen.

- The increasing baby bulge might cause discomfort and itching, which can be alleviated by letting your spouse give you a little abdominal massage. This will be beneficial in a way that your baby will start to recognize when their dad is touching your tummy. Babies have the ability to detect touch from anybody, but they also have the ability to detect whether someone's touch or voice is familiar to them by the end of your second trimester.

Engage your partner to learn about pregnancy

- Dads may have a stronger connection with the unborn if they are aware of how the baby's development is progressing and what further milestones are ahead. For example, being aware that you will begin to feel the baby kick during the second trimester and that the kicks will become more pronounced during the third trimester.

The father needs to accompany you to your prenatal appointments.

- One of the most effective strategies to initiate the father-child relationship prior to the birth of your baby is to invite the dad to come along with you to prenatal visits. He will be able to appreciate the baby's heartbeat together with you, watch the baby move on the ultrasound screen, and receive updates on their progress directly from the doctor. This will increase the bond for all three of you as a family.

Packing the Hospital Bag

When expecting a child, having mental tranquility is quite beneficial. There is a good chance that you have spent the last several months fantasizing about the day when you will finally get to meet your baby. Preparing everything and planning in advance might help ease any nerves or anxiety you may be feeling in anticipation of this joyful and life-changing occasion. This section will cover items you should include in your hospital bag to make your childbirth and recovery more comfortable. The items will include what you, your partner, and your baby need. Having the basics prepared at least three weeks before your baby's due date is essential. It is important that you be aware that if you plan to give birth vaginally, you will probably stay in the hospital for one to two days, but if you want to give birth through cesarean section, you could stay in the hospital for three to four days, provided that there are no complications.

What you need to pack:

- Proof of your identity, information regarding insurance, and hospital notes.

- Your prenatal schedule. If you have a birth plan, you should print some copies and bring them with you to the hospital. You should give one copy to your doctor, some to your labor nurse, and maybe one more to display in your hospital room. It is helpful to underline important topics so you can refer to them more easily during or after labor.

- Sanitary pads. The hospital will supply sanitary pads to absorb any blood that will be coming out as discharge after birth, but if you prefer a particular brand, you are more than welcome to bring your own. Also, ensure that you have a stock of maternal pads which are different from your regular pads.

- Comfortable clothing. Dressing postpartum requires you to be comfortable. Stay away from anything that is overly confining. Pack a nursing bra in your bag if you intend to breastfeed your baby. Pack tank tops, joggers, or lightweight sleep trousers, both of which are comfortable and loose-fitting options. Another choice is to bring along pajamas or a nightgown that is conducive to breastfeeding. A robe is also useful for postpartum recovery due to its ample comfort. It will come in handy if you give birth vaginally or by cesarean section.

- Toiletries. Remember to bring these with you just in case the hospital does not provide them. You are going to want to bring your brushes, regular shampoo, toothpaste and toothbrush, moisturizer, petroleum jelly, deodorant, hair bands, and face wipes.

- Don't forget to carry your mobile device together with its charger. You might want to carry a multi-plug outlet with you just in case you need to charge many electrical devices simultaneously.

- If you use spectacles or contacts, you shouldn't forget to pack them

- Create a music playlist, books you would like to read, or a podcast, something that will make you relax.

- If you have any massage oils or labor lotions, they can come in handy when true contractions start, and even after giving birth.

- Make sure you ask your health care provider if the snacks you want to have will be safe for you during the process. Don't rely on the healthcare facility or birthing center to supply you with snacks after the baby is born in the late hours of the night; carry your own.

Your partner needs to pack:

- Parking and vending machines require cash or your debit card, so be sure your partner has both.

- Charger and phone to keep family and close friends informed about the labor and delivery process.

- Camera. Your partner might want to take pictures and videos of the important event! Certain hospitals and birth centers do not permit videotaping of the actual birthing process; however, there is often no regulation prohibiting shooting either during labor or after the birth.

- They should carry something for entertainment. It can be a book, laptop, or headphones. Download some fresh podcasts to have on hand in the event that they find some free time.

- A different set of attire because you will likely stay in the hospital depending on what type of delivery mode you will have. Your partner will need extra clothes to change in.

- Products for personal hygiene such as toothpaste, toothbrush, deodorant, body wash, and conditioner.

- Snacks, you don't want your partner leaving you to go and look for snacks or him diving into your snacks.

- A resting bag and pillow that isn't too heavy. The pillows and linens at a hospital are often made of thin, scratchy material.

Packing for your baby:

- An outfit for going home. Because you can't predict how large or how tiny your baby will be, even though an ultra-scan can give you an idea, you should bring two or three different clothing in a range of sizes just in case. Aim to have one outfit in the size of a newborn and one in the size of 0-3 months. If the weather warrants it, you should bring a hat and socks with you.

- A receiving blanket, a few burp cloths, and additional layers like a sweater or bunting are all essential baby items.

- Carry feeding bottles if you plan to use them. If you intend to start bottle feeding immediately, bring at least one or two bottles with you to the hospital. If you intend to start your baby on formula, bring along some of your chosen formula brands, even though the hospital will probably provide it.

- Baby oil, diaper ointment, and some diapers. Even though the hospital will provide, make sure you carry yours just to be on the safe side cause you never know what can happen

- Safe car seat for your baby when going back home

Transport

Because labor can start at any time of the day or night, you should prepare to get to your birthing center in advance. If you intend to travel using your vehicle, check that it is in good operating condition and that there is sufficient fuel in the tank at all times. Make other plans in case someone who offered to take you there fails do so, even if they have already committed.

Chapter 4:

Preparing for Labor

Physically and Mentally

Talk About Your Birth Plan

Once you have reached your third trimester, your big day is so close you won't know before it's time! This is your chance to put together your birth plan. A birth plan is a record that specifies how you want your healthcare team to handle your birthing process. Some doctors may provide you with a template to fill in; others will let you lead. Although using templates as a guide can be beneficial, it is ultimately up to you to decide what information you would like to include.

Birth plans not only help instill a sense of control in you but also assist medical professionals in better comprehending your priorities for labor and the time just after that. Even though birth plans don't guarantee a certain outcome, they do provide a crystal clear framework of how you want your labor and delivery to go. You can decide how you want the process to go by putting together a clear birth plan in advance, as it lets others know your preferences for the process. You won't have to worry about such matters when the day comes. It gives you room to channel your energy toward bringing your bundle of joy into the world.

Your birth plan could include details such as whether or not you want to use pain medication, who you want by your side throughout labor, or what you want to eat on your big day. You are free to include anything you believe would ease your discomfort during labor and delivery. A birth plan includes not only a list of your preferences but also consideration of what is achievable and which of your wishes your healthcare provider and birthing center or hospital can fulfill.

Your plans for the delivery of the baby can shift as the pregnancy progresses. It is acceptable for you to change some of your decisions regarding labor and delivery. You have the right to change your mind and alter the original plan at any time. It is all about you and the baby after all.

Components of Your Birth Plan

A brief plan that outlines the essential details is simple for the people working with you to understand. Avoid the temptation of wanting to force a lot of information onto your birth plan. You can include some of the following components in your birth plan.

- essentials

o   Include your name, next of kin, your attending physician's name, the name of the place where you intend to give birth, and the names and contact information of any other individuals you would like to be there for your big day.

- medications for pain

    o   Finding effective ways to manage pain is one of the most critical considerations during labor. You might not initially intend to get an epidural, but when you're in labor, you might find yourself wanting one. I wanted to keep my process as natural as possible, so I didn't want any pain medications. Other women decide to get an epidural as long as it is feasible. Either option is acceptable; remember, this is about what makes you comfortable. Ask your healthcare provider about the various pain treatment alternatives available to you while you are still working on developing your birth plan. Don't hesitate to bring up any concerns, such as massage or deep breathing, or questions you may have about these options.

- mood

    o   Consider the factors that will contribute most to your sense of ease. Do you prefer that there be as little noise as possible in the room, or would you rather have some soft music playing? Would you prefer the lights to be turned down lower? Do you wish to document the process by having your support person shoot pictures while you are in labor?

- labor preferences

    o Suggest what would make you comfortable during labor. For instance, outline if you plan to use a birthing ball, chair, or stool throughout your labor. Do you prefer to move about unrestricted? Do you want to have a nice, warm bath before and after?

- delivery preferences

    o You have various paths to take into consideration when planning the delivery of your newborn bundle. Would having an episiotomy be okay with you if you are going to deliver vaginally, or would you rather avoid it unless it was absolutely required from a medical standpoint? Should your partner be there throughout delivery? Do you want them to cut the umbilical cord instead of the medical personnel doing it for you? Do you wish to be able to see the birth in a mirror? Do you want the medical personnel to place your newborn on your stomach immediately after the delivery? I asked them to let mine find the way to my breasts without help. Do you need help delivering the placenta, or do you intend to wait it out? I asked my medical team to wait until the placenta descended on its own. If you deliver via C-section, would you want your partner to be with you in the operating room? Is there someone else you would like to contact if it comes to that?

- aftercare preferences

    o After your tiny human arrives, you will need to decide how they will feed and what care they will receive while in the hospital. For instance, do you want to be with your baby in the room all the time, or do you feel it would be more comfortable for them to spend a few hours in the nursery? Do you plan to start breastfeeding soon after the delivery, do you intend to introduce your baby to the bottle, or perhaps you want to combine breastfeeding and bottle feeding? Are you okay with the medical personnel providing your little one with sugar water or a pacifier?

    o You and your partner can discuss your options as you draw up the birth plan. You can also share your preferences with any other individuals who will be with you during the process. Once you settle that and everything is as you wish, you can then inquire with your healthcare provider to see if they accept all your wishes. It is important to have your doctor review the birth plan ahead of time so you can figure out a way forward if they have delivery policies that do not accommodate your preferences. In such an unfortunate event, your healthcare provider will walk you through what they can and cannot do for you. Once you have all the facts straight, they will leave the decision-making up to you.

After you settle all of the details, you may have to take a copy of your birth plan to the birthing center and share another one with your doctor to preserve in your medical files. When you go into labor, it would be brilliant to carry a few copies of your birth plan in case your primary physician is unable to proceed with you and you end up with someone else.

Does preparing a birth plan sound like too much work? No one requires you to create a birth plan in advance because you can communicate your preferences with your healthcare team when you get to the hospital. Nonetheless, thinking about all your possible alternatives and discussing them with both your spouse and your doctor while you still have time is important for your peace.

Kegel Exercises

As much as exercise is important, you cannot perform just any exercises when you are pregnant. That is because not all of them are safe for you and the baby. You have to use caution when working out during this period. Avoid sports and activities that demand a significant amount of leaping, bouncing, hopping, running, or skipping because they are exhausting and have a risk of falls. Activities such as volleyball, softball, basketball, and football involve physical contact and have a high risk of injury so you should also steer clear of them when you are pregnant.

Low-impact aerobics, swimming, prenatal yoga, and light walks are some safe exercises for pregnant women. You can have an instructor help you if you prefer. These kinds of exercises will keep you fit throughout your pregnancy without raising concerns about possible injuries.

You can also try kegel exercises, also known simply as Kegels. They are a simple and excellent approach to locating and strengthening your pelvic floor muscles during pregnancy. Exercising your pelvic floor muscles supports your bladder, rectum, and uterus. A healthy pelvic floor can aid in the prevention and treatment of the following problems:

- stress urinary incontinence

- hemorrhoids

- fecal incontinence

- pelvic organ prolapse

- urgency urinary incontinence

Performing exercises targeting the pelvic floor muscles also helps tone your vaginal muscles, which can improve your sexual enjoyment during pregnancy. Kegels are easy to do, and people won't be able to tell you are exercising unless you tell them.

Imagine you are attempting to stifle the urge to pass gas or block the flow of pee from your body. It is important to use the correct technique when performing Kegels. When you are performing Kegels, you should make an effort to keep your legs, buttocks, and abdominal muscles as still as possible. Try not to tighten or squeeze adjacent muscles, such as those in your legs, buttocks, or stomach, to avoid using the wrong muscles when exercising.

Once you master the fundamentals of Kegels, you can perform them in any posture and at any time. To alternate between different postures, here are four angles that are relaxed:

- lying down

- standing

- kneeling on both hands and legs

- sitting

In order to achieve maximal strength, it is best to practice in all the four positions on a daily basis. When performing Kegel exercises, one strategy to keep in mind is to contract and release from the vagina toward the direction of your cervix.

Do You Need a Doula?

A woman who is expecting a child, is in the process of giving birth, or has just recently given birth might require some physical and emotional assistance from a trained professional who specializes in childbirth, a doula. The doula's goal is to ensure your birthing experience is not only memorable but also safe and empowering. You can think of your doula as a pregnancy support companion because they will offer you their support and educate you as necessary throughout the process.

During your birthing process, your doula's responsibility is to be a consistent source of encouragement and comfort. Your doula, as opposed to your midwife or doctor, is not trained to provide medical services. Instead, their role is to offer guidance on labor positions, breathing exercises, relaxation techniques, and other similar activities.

Before the day you are due, your doula spends some time getting acquainted with you, and vice-versa. This helps them learn how best they can support you. It also enables them to revisit some basic information for your educational purposes.

Your doula is able to provide you with suggestions about a number of non-medical strategies for pain management. These are options such as aromatherapy, mantras, massage, music, and reflexology, which can be extremely beneficial to women during labor. You and your doula will experiment with a variety of combinations until you identify the ones that work best for you.

Doulas play a vital role because they help advocate for you during a very vulnerable time in your life, such as during labor and just after that. They will assist in making sure that your healthcare team respects your preferences and does everything as agreed unless there is an inevitable medical reason to deviate from your birth plan.

Does it sound like a lot of work for the doula? Are you worried they might take your partner's place? A competent doula would never try to replace your partner. If your partner is supporting you through this difficult time or you have other people helping you, a decent doula will gladly strengthen the support you already have and may also calm other people down when they get worried.

Bear in mind that a good doula strives to make your delivery experience a safe and positive process, and their presence enables your loved ones to take a break without worrying too much about you. You can comfortably rely on them to support you because they take pleasure in doing just that.

Preterm Labor Preparation

Newborns are regarded as premature if they are born at a gestational age of 37 weeks or earlier. When you are expecting a baby who will be born prematurely or one who will have health issues, you may know those details in advance. For instance, if you will have twins, the ultrasound scans and other tests would have already shown you. The same rule applies if your unborn bundle suffers from a condition that impacts their development and overall wellness.

After the delivery, you will have a lot to do because of your new baby. You will want to be present in the neonatal intensive care unit (NICU). There are a few things you can do to prepare in the event of a difficult or early delivery. Planning ahead can be helpful in easing the burden of fitting in day-to-day responsibilities such as grocery shopping and meal preparation, which can be challenging during that time.

Ask for clarification.

- Have an open and honest conversation with your obstetrician regarding the possibility of premature labor and birth. Ask them about this possibility throughout the course of your pregnancy. Think about what would happen if you were to deliver your baby early. Navigate your options if the baby was to have complications. This is not to say you should stress yourself over the possibility of negative outcomes during your pregnancy, but productive worrying is essential for your plans. Find out if the hospital has a (NICU), what kind of care it offers, and whether or not your baby can receive treatment there. This is important because not all hospitals or birthing centers have a neonatal department to handle preterm birth and serious health issues after birth. Don't let your healthcare team get away with giving you ambiguous responses. Some may tell you to think about negative outcomes, but what would happen if it turns out your baby needs immediate extra care that the facility cannot provide? It is vital that you know what to anticipate to provide the best you can for your baby once they arrive, regardless of what state they arrive in.

Start stocking up.

- Prepare your cabinets and refrigerator with enough necessities for as far ahead as you can. Cooking some meals at home and freezing them for later consumption would be smart because cooking might become a challenge when you have to care for your newborn bundle day and night. Remember to save some room in your freezer because you will need it for storing breast milk if you are going to feed your baby human milk.

Visit the NICU.

- Find out the location of your hospital's NICU if it has one. If not, ask the healthcare team where they would transfer your baby for intensive care should the need arise. During your visit to the maternity ward, it is possible that you will receive information regarding the neonatal intensive care unit, but if they do not tell you on their own, then you should ask. While some hospital policies may allow you to enter the NICU, others won't. If the hospital where you are giving birth won't let you in, you can talk to the medical personnel to understand who would be taking care of your little one if they require intensive care.

Put together a home assistance plan.

- If you can find someone to assist you with tasks such as laundry, cleaning, ironing, food shopping, and so on, you should definitely take advantage of that opportunity. If your home stays as close to usual as it possibly can, you will experience less tension, and that will give you a greater sense of control. Remember, you won't be able to be a supermom right after delivering. For example, after having a Cesarean section, you shouldn't get behind the wheel for roughly six weeks or until your incision has completely healed. You may realize that your loved ones would be happy to lend a hand by driving you to the health care facility.

Get ready for the day.

- Consider who will accompany you to the birthing facility, remain with you, and be there as your emotional support. You will also have to prepare the luggage you want to take to the hospital. If you feel you are not ready to start packing it, you can still make a list of the items you intend to put together. Leave the list behind if you suddenly have to leave for the hospital before you have had time to finish packing, you can leave it behind, and your significant other or another support person may pack what you require at a later time. You might wish to capture pictures or films while you are in the neonatal intensive care unit. If your device is in airplane mode, you should not have any problems with this. You could also choose to bring a camera with you. You may want a journal to document the development of your baby, the changes that occur on a daily basis, and questions for the nurses and physicians. There are also apps for smartphones that might assist you in keeping up with the latest developments. It is likely that you will be required to bring clothes for the baby if you choose to deliver your little one from a private hospital.

- If you plan on having your newborn stay in a public hospital, you might not need to bring any baby clothes because the hospital will provide all your child requires. However, if your child's health has stabilized and they are able to wear clothes, you may find it more convenient to buy your own clothes for the baby. You can search in advance for shops and brands that sell clothes for premature babies. These are incredibly simple to put on and take off, and the materials used to design them are really comfortable.

Establish a chain of communication.

- It might be a lot of work to update everyone on the latest information on your newborn. Having one or two individuals who serve as the points of communication can be helpful. This setup enables y to inform the contact people about what is new at the hospital, and they will relay the information to others. Your loved ones are bound to worry because it is a big step when you go into labor. It is wise to let them know you may not be able to communicate directly with them, but your contact people will forward their messages to you. Your contact people can also share the news with other people when the baby is on its way, and you won't have to deal with that pressure.

Chapter 5

Going Into Labor—Do You Have Everything You Need?

The term *labor* describes the process at the end of pregnancy which starts with uterus contractions and then dilatation of the cervix, and ultimately these actions lead to expulsion or delivery of the baby. It took me a lot of time to research how to have a healthy, natural labor process.

I received chiropractic care to control joint and lower back pain, among its other benefits during labor. I also visited an acupuncturist, practiced some yoga, and did a lot of walking. For first-time mothers, knowing the signs that indicate the beginning of labor, things that must be done before labor starts, pushing tips, and pain medication used during labor can be very helpful in reducing stress, anxiety, and fear of the unknown.

Induction of Labor

Many of us want to go with the natural flow and let labor progress as it should, but in some instances, our bodies require a little push. Labor induction is a procedure that triggers childbirth using some techniques or medications, rather than waiting for it to start on its own. While it is possible to request labor induction for personal reasons, your doctor will only recommend it when you or the baby are at risk because of an underlying medical problem, such as in high-risk pregnancies, or the baby is not coming on its own. Whatever the reasons for your induction, they should not expose you or the baby to unnecessary risk.

Some expectant parents try to quicken labor using techniques they can perform at home. Others use approaches such as acupuncture to hurry things along. Although some parents swear by these strategies, it is important that you consult your healthcare provider before attempting any hacks, even when people describe them as "natural." You can discuss your options with reliable healthcare professionals if you want to try natural techniques to hurry labor along. Some of the techniques people use to quicken labor include nipple stimulation, eating spicy foods, having sexual intercourse, and engaging in physical exercise when they draw close to their estimated dates of delivery.

Risks of Induction

Labor induction has the potential to cause significant adverse outcomes, so it is not a choice you should make lightly. Another issue with this opinion is that there is no guarantee that inducing labor will be successful, and if it fails, you could end up needing a cesarean section. Both you and the baby may experience adverse effects due to the drugs or procedures used to induce birth.

Some of the problems that may arise with labor induction include:

- strong contractions, your part
- slow baby heart rate
- poor brain and lung development
- uterine rupture
- baby hearing and eyesight issues
- umbilical cord problems
- heavy bleeding on your part
- fetal death

- infections in both you and your newborn

Reasons to Induce

If induction can be so dangerous, why is it an option?

You may want to consider inducing labor if you have been pregnant for longer than normal or have health problems that might interfere with the pregnancy, but some do it for convenience.

Elective Induction of Labor

Those who make plans to induce pregnancy based on non-medical reasons request to have an elective induction. It is often for your convenience or for the medical team but convenience is not a recommended reason to perform induction. Examples of instances that may prompt you and your family to request elective induction include:

- if the practitioner of your choice won't be working during the days close to your estimated date of delivery, EDD

- if a member of your family is set to go somewhere far and would like to see the baby before they leave

- if you want to choose a date of birth for your baby

- if you have to undergo vigorous training or go somewhere where the pregnancy could be in danger.

Induction Prompted by Health Concerns

- If you are pregnant with twins, triplets, or decuplets—any form of multiple gestations, your unborn babies may have growth challenges in the womb, and it becomes a better option for them to grow outside.

- When your little one is still in the womb after 42 weeks of gestation, there is a chance that they may have complications meconium aspiration, seizures, or shoulder injuries.

- When you have preexisting or gestational diabetes and are having trouble managing your symptoms, your doctor may suggest that you have labor induced before week 40 to avoid issues such as a baby with an abnormally large head or stillbirth.

- If you have uncontrolled hypertension while carrying your little one, the condition can result in serious consequences such as preeclampsia so it would be best to get labor started as soon as your little one can survive outside without many complications.

- When your amniotic sac ruptures too early, your doctor may suggest induction of labor to dodge the risk of infection for you or your little one.

- If there are anatomical issues in the womb, such as a history of C-section delivery, uterine rupture, or placenta previa, your doctor may suggest induction of labor to avoid further complications.

Medical Ways of Inducing Labor

When it is necessary, your doctor may conduct induction at 39 weeks of gestation or later unless otherwise in specific instances that demand it to be done earlier.

Among the available methods for labor induction in hospital settings are:

Cervical ripening

- This technique involves triggering the cervix to dilate by using thinning and softening agents. In order to accomplish this goal, your healthcare physician may recommend the use of prostaglandins, other drugs, or a manual technique that uses an inflatable tube to expand the cervix.

Stripping membranes

- Your doctor may gently glide their finger over the membranes that are joining the amniotic sac to your uterus to stimulate the body into releasing prostaglandins and boosting natural contractions.

Amniotic sac rupture

- If your water hasn't broken on its own throughout the natural birth process, your doctor can break it to assist you in entering labor. Your healthcare professional may use a medical instrument to break your amniotic sac, the bag of water that protects your unborn baby from external harm. The procedure is known as an amniotomy.

Labor induction is not a guaranteed approach; sometimes, these methods fail. In such instances, you may go home and then return later to give it another shot, or your doctor may suggest you opt for a Cesarean section if it becomes necessary.

Signs of Labor

Labor is a process that involves expelling products of conception, including your baby and placenta. For your baby and the placenta to exit from your womb, delivery can be through your vagina or a surgical operation. It's been months of carrying your little bundle of joy inside you, and it's almost time. Finding out what the symptoms of labor are might make you feel more prepared for the labor and delivery process as your due date draws nearer.

Lightening is a sign that labor is close. When the position of the baby in your pelvis changes, they drop lower as this phenomenon is known as lighting. It indicates that your baby is getting ready to shift into the appropriate position for delivery. It can happen a few weeks or even a few hours before your labor begins. If you are wondering how to know when your baby has dropped, there is no definite answer because it varies from one woman to another. Some women don't even notice or feel anything, others feel there is some space that has been created in the abdomen, and breathing becomes more manageable. When lightening occurs, the pressure on your stomach eases, and that helps reduce heartburn. In some instances, you might feel as though you are carrying a ball in your pelvis. You can carry out light activities to encourage your baby to drop.

So now, how would you know that you are now in labor?

When you start experiencing labor, one of the first things you will feel is contractions. Contractions are caused by muscles of the uterus tightening up and relaxing, this is to get ready to evict your baby out of the uterus; as a result, you experience abdominal pain and cramps. Contractions are strong, regular, and sustained. When you are in real labor, your contractions will typically last between 30 to 60 seconds and occur at 5 to 10 minutes intervals. They are so powerful that you will be unable to walk or communicate while they are occurring. Over time, they become stronger and closer to one another.

Contractions also create a change in the shape of your cervix. Your cervix will start dilating (widening) and flattening to make it favorable for birth; this indicates that labor has begun for you. The baby will be expelled from the uterus with the assistance of contractions. The entrance that leads to the uterus is called the cervix, and it is located at the top of the vagina.

Another sign that mostly goes hand in hand with contractions is bloody show. This is a discharge of mucus and blood, which might be brownish or reddish in color. This discharge will be coming out from your vagina.

You are experiencing discomfort in both your stomach and lower back. This discomfort does not go away even when you shift positions or move around. You will also have the urge to go to the toilet.

Your water breaks. Your child has been developing in the amniotic fluid that is contained within your uterus.

What is false labor, and what are Braxton Hicks contractions?

While we talked about contractions as a crucial sign of labor, there are specific contractions that may not indicate that you are in labor. It's possible to experience these contractions even when true labor hasn't started. This is called false labor or Braxton-Hicks contractions. Braxton-Hicks contraction assists in preparing the cervix for labor by making it more pliable. It's possible that you'll start to feel them in the weeks leading up to your due date. Understanding the distinctions between true labor contractions and false labor contractions will help you determine whether you are actually in true labor.

It is not always easy to distinguish the difference between real labor and false labor but let's break down how you can distinguish the two, false labor or Braxton Hicks contractions are not regular and sustained, this means that they are not consistent and have an irregular pattern compared to true labor contractions which are regular and sustained. One thing that can help is timing your contractions as soon as you feel them. Record the amount of time that elapses between the beginning of one contraction and the beginning of the following one in the space provided. Take careful note of the intensity of the contractions as they occur. Maintain a log of your contractions for the next 30 minutes to an hour. Another thing you need to take note of is that true labor contractions become stronger as time goes on while false labor contractions do not increase in intensity. Also, be on the lookout for other signs like bloody discharge and water breaking. Don't hesitate to check in with your healthcare provider if you are experiencing strong contractions that are regular and increasing in intensity.

Call your health care provider immediately, regardless of the time of day or night, if you believe that you are entering the labor process. If you need to go to the hospital, your physician will let you know when it's time to go. Your health care practitioner will examine and measure your cervix to confirm that you are indeed in the laboring stage.

What to do Before Going into Labor

You are probably wondering and panicking, not knowing what to do before labor. Do not worry, a list of things needs to be sorted out to make it easier for you when the baby arrives.

Attend classes about giving birth.

- You may prepare yourself for the fundamentals of labor by reading up on them in advance, but it is more beneficial to work on breathing and relaxation methods with someone who is experienced in the field. Professionals will help you get better prepared, and you can ask all your questions.

Get familiar with labor contractions.

- It can be difficult as a first-time mom to recognize that you are having a contraction and it's not any other cramp. Luckily contractions have been covered in signs of labor and how you can distinguish true and false labor.

Get familiar with the fundamentals of nursing babies.

- Do not anticipate that your baby will immediately latch on and begin eating. It will be a process of learning for both of you, and as a first-time mother, you will face some difficulties. Educating yourself about the fundamentals before giving birth may eliminate as many potential frustrations and fatigue. You will be mentally and physically prepared by getting familiar with the fundamentals.

Purchase a baby bed and prepare the rest of the nursery.

- Every baby has a fundamental requirement for a secure sleeping environment: Before your baby comes in, make sure that you have purchased and thoroughly assembled the baby's bed and followed the steps in this checklist to create a secure and functional nursery.

Prepare your luggage for the hospital.

- Before traveling to the hospital, check that you have all the necessary items in your possession. A section in Chapter 3 covers the list you need.

Leave your house in order.

- You have the inclination to start a family. At this point, you should focus on getting your house in order so that it is ready for the arrival of your child. You can participate in activities that are not strenuous but do not stress or exhaust yourself. You can ask your partner or family and friends to help you with this.

Learn to spot the warning signs.

- If you see any of the following symptoms at any point throughout your pregnancy, including when you are in labor or at any other time, you should immediately contact your healthcare practitioner or a clinic:

- The fluid that comes from your vagina, whether or not contractions are present.

- Experiencing strong enough bleeding to require the use of a sanitary pad

- Discomfort in your pelvis that is severe or pain that is constant in your abdomen or back

- Fever or temperature that is more than 37.5 degrees

- Nausea or vomiting that does not go away, occurs more than three times a day, or the inability to tolerate food or drinks for more than 24 hours

- Alterations in eyesight that came on all of a sudden (blurring, double vision, seeing spots)

- Inability to pass feces after three to four days, particularly if accompanied by acute pelvic discomfort

- Urinary discomfort or difficulty, particularly if accompanied by blood in the urine or a significantly reduced volume of urine passed during the day.

- Fainting episodes or persistent dizziness

Pushing Tips to Try

Now that you have reached labor, it's time to push the baby out. Each woman feels different at this point, you may either feel relieved to start pushing, embarrassed, frustrated, scared, or inhibited. All these feelings are normal, and every woman experiences them in a unique way.

The best way to begin pushing is to move into a pushing position of your choice. Pushing is usually done three times per contraction or as the urge comes. Hospital practitioners or birthing center staff will help guide you as you push. When you get tired, you may get some rest for one contraction.

While you push, it helps to think of it as moving your bowels as hard as you can, though sometimes, as you push, you may empty your bowels or urinate during the process. That's very normal and occurs to almost every woman. Remember that the staff assigned to you has had experience with handling women in labor and is aware of emptying of bowels and urine during this process. Push without any hesitation or worry about emptying your bowels.

Putting your chin to your chest helps you focus your pushes to exactly where they need to be. You can only tuck your chin if you are propped up on your back. As you tuck your chin to your chest, looking at your navel can also give a great deal of focus as it reminds you where the pushes should come from

As you push, make sure each push is to the best of your abilities. Push with all your might in order to assist the baby in moving along the birth canal. The harder you push, the faster the baby moves. Avoid panicking while pushing, but instead, maintain control.

Change positions if your baby isn't moving down the canal as you push.

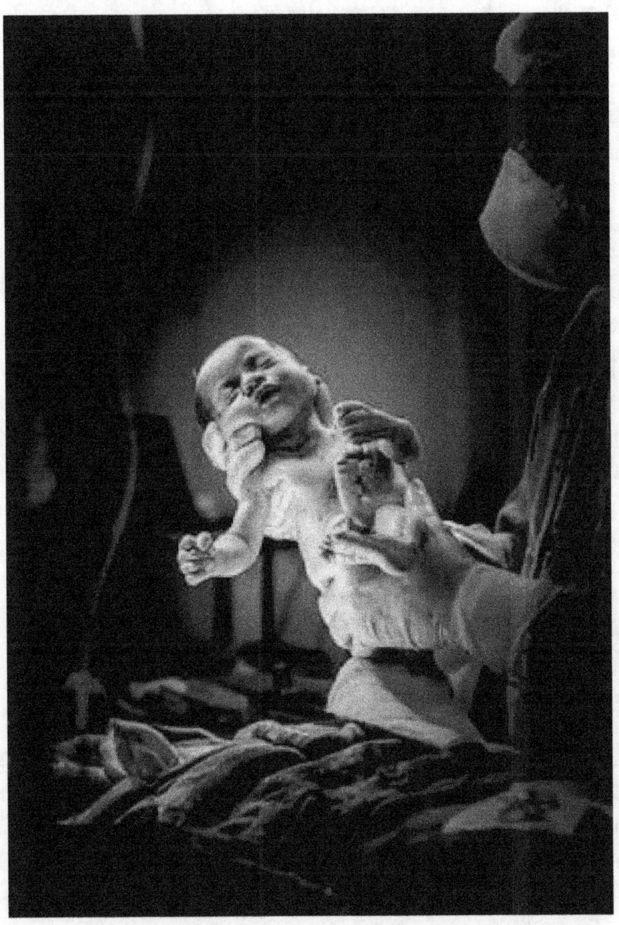

There are a number of ways you can push, but what's important is to follow what feels right to you. You can either push based on your urge or push as directed by asking the staff to count up to ten before each push. Not all women have the urge to push during labor, and that's normal. You can breathe in as much as possible while the next contraction builds up, breathe in as deep as possible once the contraction reaches its peak, and then push as hard as possible.

As you begin to lose strength, your practitioner may advise that you rest and skip pushing for a couple of contractions. Another reason to stop pushing is to keep the baby's head from coming out too fast. You can pant or bow instead of pushing.

You can also try touching your baby's head during crowning or looking at it because that can motivate you to push even harder. Though motivation can come from touching or looking at your baby's head, you must remember that it's also natural for your baby's head to disappear as you push once crowning has happened, do not be discouraged because it's all part of the process.

Pain Management

Labor *is* a challenging experience, and we often struggle with the idea of its pain. Although the level of tolerance differs greatly from one woman to another, we would all experience some degree of pain if we did not use tricks to lessen or numb the pain. Some women stand against using other forms of medical assistance to reduce or stop pain during labor. Others are content and eager to investigate all of their available choices.

First-time labor can be a little unpredictable, so it is ideal to know some of the many strategies available for alleviating pain and the possible risks they come with.

Non-Medical Pain Management During Labor and Delivery

Below are some nonmedical methods that may help you cope with labor pain:

- knowing what to expect throughout the process

- trying hypnosis, acupuncture, and acupressure

- getting a massage

- having constant support

- using hot or cold packs

- staying in a warm bath or getting a warm shower

- using distractions such as music

- exercising breathing techniques

- maintaining physical activity

Epidural

This method of pain management is another form of local anesthetic. An epidural is not supposed to make you feel nauseous or sleepy. In almost all circumstances, an epidural will provide total pain relief when it dulls the nerves from carrying pain sensations to the brain. If it's your first time, you may have had a lot of people tell you about the pain of childbirth, and you could be scared too. In such cases, getting an epidural can be of great assistance because it tends to work like magic, but not all women want to get rid of the pain. Many want to experience it; they may feel as though stopping the pain is eliminating the whole essence of childbirth. My plan was no epidural, but after 38 hours of labor, I caved in! In the end, it comes down to your personal preference. Although getting an epidural offers very strong pain relief, it is not always guaranteed to have 100% effectiveness in labor. Some expectant mothers may still require the assistance of other pain control measures.

If you want to go with an epidural, you won't be able to get one at home or at small facilities because the medication can only be administered by an anesthesiologist. Some local birthing centers might not offer this option because not all of them have the qualified personnel for it, so even if you tried, you would need dosage adjustments that other people on your team are not specialized to do. With that, it is vital that you check to see if there is usually an anesthesiologist at the hospital of your choice and if you have any reason to believe that you could require an epidural. Another critical thing to know is that your little one's heart rate must be monitored during and after you receive an epidural. The technology they use to monitor the heart rate is called telemetry, and the majority of hospitals do not have the proper equipment to perform it.

The amount of leg movement you have after having an epidural depends on the type of local anesthetic that was administered. Certain hospitals provide "mobile" epidurals that allow you to move around freely after receiving the injection. You can inquire with your midwife regarding the availability of mobile epidurals in your chosen hospital.

Getting an epidural to reduce pain during labor and delivery can come with some unintended consequences. Depending on the type of local anesthetic that your anesthesiologist used, you may have a heaviness in your legs, or experience hypotension, a drop in blood pressure. Not every woman experience hypotension because the fluid that the medical personnel administer through the drip during this process helps to keep the blood pressure normal.

It is possible for the epidural to extend the second stage of labor. When you are no longer having contractions, your midwife will instruct you when to begin pushing. If the baby is not exhibiting any indications of distress, the medical team will wait longer for the baby's head to drop before you start pushing. When your cervix is completely dilated, but you are pushing without progress, a ventouse or forceps may be necessary to assist in the delivery of the baby. This procedure is called instrumental delivery and is done to help your labor progress with minimal risk. Toward the end of the procedure, your team may use less anesthetic so you can feel the urge to push the baby out on your own.

As a side effect of the epidural, you might experience a headache, or your back may be a little sore for a day or two after getting an epidural. Not every woman gets a headache after receiving an epidural for labor, and the back soreness does not develop into a serious back condition, so you would be fine in a few days. You may also have trouble passing urine. If that is the case, your team may insert a thin tube known as a catheter into your bladder so you can relieve the bladder.

Remifentanil

You can take charge of your pain! After your medical team venously administers remifentanil into your arm, it can be controlled by pushing a button. You can use this drug right up until the delivery of your tiny human because it takes effect rapidly but loses its effectiveness shortly after administration. Remifentanil may cause you to feel short of breath, your medical team will need to assess your oxygen levels using a pulse oximeter they will put on your finger.

Pethidine

Your medical team will inject pethidine on your buttock or thigh to provide pain relief and help you relax during labor. It takes effect approximately twenty minutes after being injected. If your medical team gives you pethidine too close to your baby's time of birth, it may interfere with the little one's breathing. Because the effects of this medication can continue for up to four hours, it is not ideal to use it when you are in the second phase of labor and are pushing. If you get pethidine too late and it disrupts the baby's breathing, the medical team will give you a different drug to counteract the effect. Pethidine also has the potential to make you feel dizzy, forgetful, and nauseous. Another problem with this drug is how it may cause issues with your newborn's initial feeding. Otherwise, it is safe and effective for pain reduction during the painful process of labor.

Chapter 6:

The "Fourth" Trimester—

Postpartum Days

Feeding Methods

Are you going to bottle feed or breastfeed? It's up to you!

Bottle Feeding

Whether you bottle-feed your little one or opt to breastfeed is a personal choice. Deciding on feeding options is one of the significant choices you will have to make after becoming a mom. Some moms receive criticism for opting to bottle feed their babies instead of feeding them straight from the breasts. Each method has positives and negatives, so whatever you do, ignore the harsh criticism from other people. None of the options is entirely wrong, so you should make the decision that will be the best for your situation and your baby's health. When deciding whether to go with one option or the other, you need to weigh the benefits of each over their respective disadvantages.

Bottle feeding is when you give your baby milk from your breasts through a bottle or feed them formula through a bottle. If you give your baby breastmilk using a bottle, it still has the same nutrients as the milk you give directly from your breasts. The major difference is that bottle feeding provides you with more flexibility when the baby does not have to depend solely on your availability for feeding. Many new mothers who cannot breastfeed their little ones or those who combine breast milk with formula opt to bottle-feed their children. Some mothers even use bottles to serve expressed breast milk so their tiny bundles can get used to that. If you are a new mother who is thinking about giving your baby formula through a bottle, you may first want to read about the benefits and drawbacks of giving a baby formula through a bottle so that you can make a proper decision.

Here are a number of advantages of giving your baby the bottle:

Your baby can feed in public.

- If you are like some mothers who feel uncomfortable with breastfeeding their bundles in public, you can go for the bottle instead.

Bottle feeding helps keep your private spot covered without interfering with the availability of milk for your baby.

The baby won't starve when you are busy.

- Another advantage of bottle feeding is that your partner can also give the baby milk. You can spend a few hours busy or away from home without worrying about the baby feeling hungry. Breastfeeding eliminates the potential for your partner to form a deep relationship with the tiny human, but the bottle gives room for father-child bonding while feeding. Other members of your family can also spend quality time with the baby when it's time to feed.

You can easily keep a record of how much milk your little one drinks in a day.

- If you go with breastfeeding, it can be difficult to estimate the amount of milk your baby takes in at any given time. If you use the bottle, however, you will be able to more accurately gauge their daily consumption and stay alert in case their intake drastically reduces.

The bottle is handy if you are unable to breastfeed.

- You can use the bottle to feed your baby in the event that you develop an illness after giving birth. The same advantage applies if you experience other health challenges that prevent you from breastfeeding.

You can bottle-feed the baby when your milk supply is low.

- In the first few days after birth, you may realize that your milk supply is low. Although that is common, it is still worrying because mothers want their babies to feed well. In such a situation, you can rely on bottle feeding. This guarantees that your newborn bundle consumes the appropriate amount of milk for optimal growth and development.

Bottle feeding works even if your baby has trouble digesting lactose.

- In extremely unusual instances, some newborns are born with lactose intolerance, a condition that makes them unable to digest either breast milk or milk from other animals. If your baby has lactose intolerance, you can bottle-feed them healthy formula milk, such as soy protein.

You don't need to force yourself to modify your eating habits.

- If you give your little one formula milk instead of breast milk, you won't need to stress about cutting off certain foods from your diet or including some fruits and vegetables.

Disadvantages of Bottle Feeding

Preparing formula or expressing breast milk for use in a bottle requires a lot of work and time.

When it's time to feed your little one, you will need to clean and sterilize the bottle before filling it with milk. You also have to check the temperature a zillion times or risk burning your baby's tongue! If you do not sterilize your bottle-feeding equipment well, you risk your baby's wellness as there are always tons of bacteria waiting for such mistakes.

Not all babies do well with formula milk.

- We cannot argue the fact that breast milk tastes way better than formula. Your tiny human wants the good stuff too! Some babies simply don't want the formula and will make it a point by spitting it just to spend the rest of that feeding break crying. There are also other babies whose bodies do not welcome formula milk. Such babies may throw up often or suffer from diarrhea as a result of drinking formula.

Formula milk is less nutritious compared to breast milk.

- Your baby won't eat or drink anything else apart from milk and necessary medications during the first six months of their life but they will require nutrients for growth and development. Formula milk will keep your baby alive, but breast milk has all the nutrients that are necessary for your little one's growth and development.

Bottle feeding can be costly.

- Opting to bottle feed your little one can be quite pricey because it requires you to purchase extra items such as cleaning brushes, feeding bottles, a sterilizer, and a breast pump. All these items plus a lot of formula milk will end up being an additional charge on your monthly bill.

Breastfeeding

Learning how to breastfeed might sound funny and maybe even unnecessary, but it is important—I had to take a breastfeeding course!

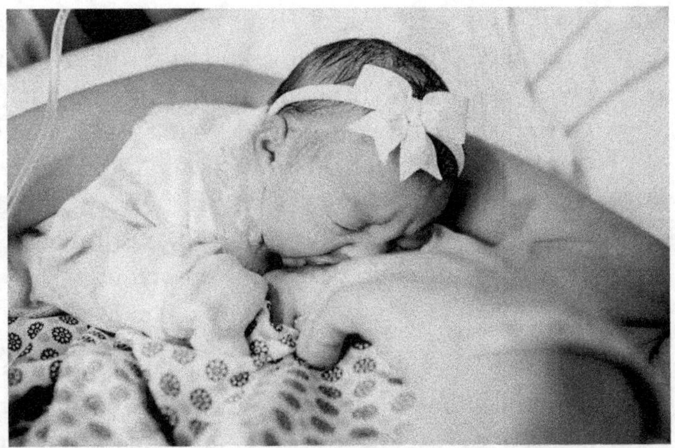

Both you and your little one gain from breastfeeding in a number of important ways. This method is not only natural, but also the healthiest approach to nourishing your newborn with all the nutrients they need for growth.

Some of the most important advantages of breastfeeding:

It is beneficial to your wellness.

- Giving your baby milk directly from your breasts may help lower your chance of developing ovarian and breast cancer. Breastfeeding mothers typically recover from the effects of delivery more quickly than those who opt to bottle feed their little ones.

It is good for your baby's health.

- Your newborn bundle will receive numerous advantages from breastfeeding in terms of their health and development. Breast milk contains a variety of natural substances that help shield your tiny human from infections and illnesses while they are young. Even after the weaning, those natural substances will continue to improve your child's overall well-being.

- In addition, your newborn will have little to no trouble digesting breast milk. That is because the milk that your body produces is already tailored to the needs of your little one. It is more easily digested than formula milk and may lower your baby's risk of developing constipation and diarrhea. It is more easily digested than formula milk and may lower your baby's risk of developing constipation and diarrhea.

Breast milk is flavorful.

Breast milk has a flavor that is considerably more unique and, in many people's opinions, superior to that of formula. Mother's milk is sweet and creamy. Additionally, the flavors of the foods that you consume are transferred to your milk, which might help train your baby to eat a more varied diet in advance. Breastfeeding also provides your little one with warmth and security. When they are hurt, ill, or upset, your baby may find comfort in breastfeeding.

Nursing saves money in the long run.

- If you want to breastfeed your child exclusively, you won't have to spend money on baby formula or bottles. Breastfeeding will also save you money by helping keep your child healthy and minimizing medical expenses.

Breastfeeding delays menstruation.

- If you breastfeed your baby, you may not have to worry about getting your period again for three to six months. Other women will go even longer without menstruating as long as their babies drink breast milk. Lactational amenorrhea can serve as a birth control method. The lactational amenorrhea technique (LAM) works if you meet the following conditions:

    o you do not supplement your breastfeeding with formula or anything else

    o your baby is less than six months old

If your menstruation has already returned, then this natural form of birth control will not work.

Breastfeeding is easier and faster than bottle feeding.

- When you breastfeed your little one, you won't have to wake up in the middle of the night to prepare and heat up bottles. This allows you time to rest while you bond with your bundle of joy. Another aspect that makes breastfeeding easy is that you don't have to worry about the milk being too hot. It is also unnecessary to bother about cleaning bottles for your baby's formula.

Disadvantages of Breastfeeding

Despite its many advantages, breastfeeding may still not be the ideal option for you and your little one. The following are some of the reasons mothers decide against natural feeding.

- Revealing your breasts to feed the baby can be embarrassing.

Many first-time mothers tend to feel awkward when they have to breastfeed their babies in front of other people. Even if you are wearing clothes that allow you to breastfeed comfortably, it can still be a little embarrassing. Because it may be difficult for you to go out in public with your little one, you may end up isolating yourself from gatherings to avoid feeling ashamed.

- Breastfeeding can be painful.

You may find yourself having to cope with pain when breastfeeding. If your tiny human does not bite you with their gums, you could feel pain from breast engorgement, sore nipples, or mastitis.

- Your partner can't help with feeding.

Breastfeeding tends to exclude your partner from the bonding process and requires you to devise other bonding strategies for your baby and the father.

- Breastfeeding gives you less room for freedom.

If you pick breastfeeding over bottle feeding, you will have to be available at all times. This means you also have to prepare for exhausting days and nights during the first few days after delivery.

- Breastfeeding for the first time is not a straightforward task.

There is no guarantee that a little one will successfully suck milk right away. Your baby will need time to get used to the whole feeding process, and their on and off sucking style can leave you feeling disheartened.

- Breastfeeding means you have to mind your diet.

Just like when you were pregnant, breastfeeding means you stay away from drugs and substances. The laws of breastfeeding require you to mind the foods you eat and the way you live your life to protect your little one from possible adverse reactions.

Adjusting to the New Normal

We sometimes have difficulties attending to our needs when it is just us that needs to be taken care of. It gets worse when you add a tiny human to the list that requires your undivided attention. Now that the game is no longer about you and you and your partner alone, things can get hectic pretty fast. You will need a lot of learning, planning, and sacrifice in order to be the best version of a mother for your little bundle. We have covered feeding, so that's a start, but you still have other headaches such as bathing the baby, handling visitors, dressing the baby, medications, and many similar issues.

Learning and Adjusting

Babies need gentle care; newborns make you walk on eggs! I didn't want to make mistakes or break my little one's fragile bones, so I also took an infant CPR and safety course.

Sleeping

First-time motherhood would be easier if we could get our newborns to sleep when we need them to.

Unfortunately, babies come with their own sleep patterns, and they don't care if their schedule is not conducive for us. The primary reason for this is that newborns have relatively small stomachs; thus, they have to eat anywhere from eight to twelve times a day, including during the night. As your baby grows, they begin to sleep less, but they still know they are your weakness, so they will keep you up when you want to sleep. Not all babies cry uncontrollably at night; some babies just want to feed, and others want you to hold them until they sleep. Try sleeping close to your little one so they know they are not alone. Being near your baby when it is time to sleep does not mean you should put them to sleep on your bed, but you can at least share the same room until your baby is older. Sharing the bed with your little one is bad for them as they can suffocate.

Feeding

Pick a comfortable position when feeding the baby. You are free to feed your little one in any favorable position. You can take a seat or lie down. You just have to make sure the feeding position you choose allows you to meet your little one's requirements without overwhelming you. Comfortable positions depend on how old your little bundle is, what time it is, who else is with you, and where you are. For example, you wouldn't want to make your newborn sit straight while you feed because at that stage, their back is not yet strong enough, and they have not yet acquired that skill. You can try the cradle hold when feeding your baby. It involves you sitting up straight with your baby in your arms. The cradle enables you to carry your tiny human in one hand while using the other to support your breast, so it does not cover the nose and suffocate the baby.

Observe the feeding. It is important that you check on your little one as they feed. If you are breastfeeding, you want to ensure your baby is sucking without difficulties, the breast is not interfering with the process, and the milk is still coming out. Your little human enjoys the milk but might not be able to give you a signal when it is no longer coming out or when they want to switch to the other breast. Ensure your little one has lips pursed around the nipple as they feed, listen for swallowing sounds and look for gestures of enjoyment such as kicking their legs about.

Always support their head while holding them to feed. That is because your little one lacks the ability to do so themself, and improper support could cause them to have neck injuries, apart from the obvious discomfort. You will also need proper physical support when nursing your baby. You can use pillows to support your back or arms. The extra support helps avoid untimely exhaustion and ensures you hold your baby up throughout the feeding process.

Diapering

We may not enjoy changing diapers, but it is an unavoidable part of the journey, so learning how to do it properly will help you in the long run. Even if you have support people offering to do it for you all the time, it is still important that you learn. You have a wide selection of brands to choose which diapers you will go with for your baby. Different brands offer varying combinations of characteristics and prices, but the fundamental purpose and steps involved in putting a diaper on your baby are the same.

You first need to get some wipes, diaper cream, baby powder, and a new diaper. Putting everything in place before you start helps you avoid leaving your baby half-dressed or unattended while you go looking for something. Lay your baby on a flat surface. Some people have a dedicated space for changing diapers, but others do it wherever is conducive at the moment. Ensure the spot you picked is safe and has enough room to keep your little one from falling off. Once everything is ready, undo the used diaper and allow your baby to take a breath before you proceed, in case they are still using the diaper—you don't want custard on your clothes!

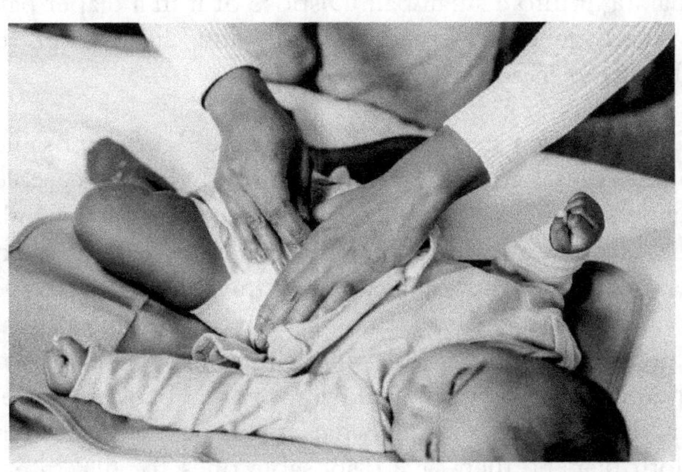

Carefully elevate your baby's bottom while holding them by the legs, then wipe if their diaper was only wet with urine. Rather than raising your baby's legs, you can gently move them to one side, clean them, then do the same on the other side. If the baby has more than just urine, try using the unspoiled part of the diaper to clean up some of the feces before using wipes to remove leftover dirt and leave your baby's bottom fresh again. This method helps you save a million wipes compared to leaving everything for the wipes. Place the used wipes on the soiled diaper before replacing it with a clean one.

Position the fresh diaper over your baby's bottom, apply your diapering products, then fasten it, making sure it's not too loose or too tight. If your baby's umbilicus still hasn't fallen, clean it well and remember not to cover it with the diaper. Finish up by dressing the baby, then crisscross the old diaper's fasteners, making it into a small ball. Dispose of it in a diaper pail or garbage can. Use fresh water and disinfectant to clean your hands after diapering.

Other women use cloth diapers instead of disposable ones. You can save money by opting for reusable diapers, but they also have their disadvantages. Cloth diapers require effort and time to clean for the next usage and may not be ideal when traveling. If you want to beat costs and still enjoy a convenient option, you can use both disposable and cloth diapers. You can spend a few days studying your baby's bowel movements to determine what time is best to give them cloth diapers, then save disposable ones for nighttime, journeys, and busy days.

Bathing

Babies enjoy the refreshing effects of a warm bath just as we do. Take some time to learn fundamental tips for bathing your newborn. Don't forget to engage them in conversation during their bath. You obviously don't expect your little one to talk back while you bathe them, but they have their way of communicating during this stage. Your bundle of joy may hold your gaze, coo, or smile at you. These gestures are signs that your baby feels safe and secure.

As always, the first step you should take is to make sure you are well-prepared. Put together your baby's washcloth, soap, towel lotion, and a fresh diaper. Always make sure the water is at the right temperature, so you don't accidentally burn the baby. When testing if the water is not too hot, you can use your elbows or wrists instead of palms to avoid misjudging. This is because the skin on wrists and elbows is softer than that on the palms.

Take your baby's clothes off with caution, being mindful of both their body and the cold. If you are too slow, your baby will feel cold and might start crying, but if you are too fast, you might hurt them since their body is still fragile. Your baby does not need to bathe every day, so you can try giving them sponge baths between days of standard baths, especially during the first few weeks of their life.

Put your little one in the bathtub, but remember to keep at least one hand on them at all times for their protection. Using a washcloth, begin with your baby's face, neck, and hair before washing the diaper area. That is because the bottom always has more dirt and feces carry bacteria that you do not want getting close to your little one's upper body.A variety of baby soaps are suitable for their hair, so you do not have to worry about their hair becoming dry or anything like that. You can also choose not to use soap on your baby's sensitive skin. When you are through with the bathing process, place your tiny human on a towel and dry them off. You can then apply moisturizer and put their diaper on. Dress your little one in fresh clothes and put them down so you can clean up.

Getting Support

Some women despise being in need of anything. They don't ask for help because they think it makes them look weak, and others fear the feeling of being indebted to the people around them but tell you what—seeking help makes us human. It is not awkward for you to ask for help from other people—what's weird is you not asking when you need assistance!

Chapter 7:

How to Take Care of Your Mental Health Post-Labor

Understanding Postpartum Depression

Depression is a mood condition that is characterized by ongoing loneliness, sorrow, and lack of joy for a prolonged period of more than two weeks. It is not the same as the usual ups and downs in mood that you go through as a normal routine of your life. Postpartum refers to the period of time beginning shortly after a woman has given birth and continuing for up to six weeks. Postpartum depression, also known as PPD, is a form of depression that develops in a new mother within the first six weeks after giving birth. Women who suffer from postpartum depression have a variety of complicated changes in their bodies, emotions, and behaviors. It is essential that you are aware that clinical depression has been cited as the primary factor in people's inability to work.

The rapid changes in sex hormones and thyroid hormone levels after delivery may significantly impact your mood and may contribute to peripartum depression. Estrogen, a sex hormone, decreases, which will result in levels of serotonin (a feel-good hormone) decreasing, and this will result in signs of depression showing in an individual. If progesterone levels are low after giving birth, another sex hormone, can cause anxiety and disturbed sleep patterns. Additionally, another hormone that helps with metabolism and body activity, Thyroid hormone, may decrease, and this can cause feelings of tiredness and slowness.

Other aspects of those at risk of having PPD are as follows: Women who have:

- a family background of mood disorders

- had depression during their current or past pregnancy

- reproductive issues or labor and delivery difficulties

- had traumatic experiences

- are grieving the death of their loved one

- financial and career problems

- environmental stress

Women who are more prone to suffer from postpartum depression are those who have unfavorable ideas about themselves as moms. In addition, some moms set impossible standards for themselves and believe they should be flawless. New moms sometimes find themselves short on personal time; as a result, they may struggle to discover their own identity and may even believe that they lack attractiveness. These overpowering sentiments might make it difficult for mothers to get a good night's sleep. If you as a first-time mother, are not getting enough sleep or any quality sleep, you may find it challenging to deal with even the most basic of issues. It's possible that you'll have the impression that you have lost control of your life, which may ultimately cause you to question your capacity to provide for your newborn children.

Postpartum Depression and Baby Blues

The baby blues are something that a lot of new mothers experience in the first week after giving birth. The baby blues are distinct from postpartum depression in that they typically only last for two to three days or less than two weeks and are not particularly severe. In contrast, postpartum depression lasts for more than two weeks and is severely debilitating, making it difficult to carry out activities of daily living. Women who have more severe symptoms or continue for more than two weeks after giving birth should be examined for postpartum depression by their healthcare provider.

Signs and Symptoms of PPD

Despair, a diminishing interest in things that were before enjoyable, lack of interest in taking care of the newborn, melancholy, unpredictable shifts in mood, sleep impairment, weak appetite, inability to focus or make judgments in a timely manner, irritation, isolation, infant, Challenges in keeping ties with others, discomfort in the body, specifically in the muscles, uncontrolled weeping, feeling of guilt, suicidal ideation, anxiety, or episodes of panic and a sense of being unable to cope are all symptoms.

In most cases, the onset of symptoms occurs gradually over a period of three months; however, it can sometimes occur suddenly. Depression that develops after delivery can make it difficult for you as a new mother to care for yourself as well as your infant.

How exactly is the diagnosis made?

Please take note that this is not meant to be a medical book, and professional help should be sorted, so don't make self-diagnosis, but this is for educational purposes. As mentioned before, seek medical advice if you or someone you know is experiencing the symptoms that were mentioned. One can be diagnosed with postpartum depression if they have had at least five symptoms for more than two weeks.

These symptoms can include:

- reduced capacity for concentration and mental clarity

- a depressed mood or a loss of pleasure

- significant weight loss or gain

- agitation or slowdown of cognitive and motor processes

- insomnia or hypersomnia

- a sense of not being good enough or of guilt

- loss of appetite

- thoughts of self-harm, murder, or both.

You will be asked about how you feel, so don't think it is weird. You have to open up to the medical care provider. Some tests will be performed by your doctor in order to rule out any other potential health problems that could be the cause of the symptoms. For instance, a decrease in thyroid hormones can mimic symptoms of depression. If all of the criteria for postpartum depression are satisfied, then a diagnosis of the condition can be made after all other potential causes of symptoms have been eliminated.

It's possible that some women won't admit to experiencing signs of depression due to cultural and societal issues; thus, health care practitioners are going to question you about your antepartum and postpartum feelings.

Treatment of PPD

Women who are experiencing mild to moderate depression symptoms may benefit from treatment techniques that do not include the use of pharmaceutical drugs. Effective psychotherapies include cognitive-behavioral and interpersonal therapy, which can be delivered either individually or in groups. Additionally beneficial might be support groups. When it comes to taking care of your mental health following the birth of your baby, these techniques may be especially appealing if you are breastfeeding and desire to avoid using medication.

If your condition does not respond well to counseling and non-drug treatment, or if your symptoms of depression range from mild to severe, then your doctor will consider pharmacologic treatment options. Antipsychotic and antidepressant medication may be used in cases with both types of symptoms. Even though some antidepressant drugs are passed through breast milk, the majority of SSRIs (A group of antidepressant drugs) and mood stabilizers are considered safe for breastfeeding. However, it is important to keep a close eye on your baby while you are taking these medications. It is possible that the medicine should be stopped if your little one demonstrates signs of irritation, trouble feeding, or sleep disturbance as a result of medication. It is important to have open communication with your doctor in order to determine the most appropriate course of therapy for you.

Complications Associated With PPD

The emotional and logistical demands of caring for a newborn and family might cause a partner of a woman with postpartum depression to feel overwhelmed. It may also be distressing for them to see their spouse struggle with postpartum depression (PPD), which will likely cause the couple's connection to become strained. It is essential to be aware that paternal postpartum depression (PPD) is a real possibility. Some partners experience symptoms such as weariness as well as changes in their food or sleeping patterns. It is anticipated that some men will experience symptoms of depression within the first year of being a father. Younger dads who suffered from depression in the past and fathers who are struggling financially are more likely to experience depression than older fathers or other fathers.

Postpartum depression (PPD) patients who do not receive therapy run the risk of developing severe depression. There is a possibility that you will struggle to form a relationship with your young one. As a result, you will have an increased likelihood of failing to thrive, excessive crying, poor nutrition, inadequate sleep, and developmental delays as a result of their conditions. Suicide, infanticide (infant homicide), and physical injury to your baby are possible outcomes of untreated postpartum depression (PPD).

A mother's mentality and actions toward her child have a major impact not just on the relationship that forms between the mother and child but also on the child's overall health and growth. Moms who suffer from depression are more likely to display poor facial relations and have difficulty interacting with their infants. These mothers may withdraw more or behave in an overly invasive manner. In addition, women who are experiencing signs of depression are more likely to stop nursing earlier in the postpartum period than other moms.

If you suffer from postpartum depression, your child is most likely to display behavioral problems such as difficulties sleeping, eating, anger outbursts, overactivity, delays in intellectual growth, emotional and social withdrawals, and possible depressive disorders.

Children of mothers who do not suffer from depression are less likely to exhibit these symptoms. In addition to this, if you have PPD, your child will tend to have somewhat faster rates of weight growth during the first six months of their lives, which may be an indicator of an increased likelihood of obesity in later years.

What is the prognosis of PPD?

The symptoms may go away on their own for some people. Some people are able to rid themselves of their symptoms with the help of medicine, psychotherapy, or a combination of the two. After around six months of therapy, the majority of moms report feeling better.

Benefits of Seeking Counseling During Postpartum

As a new mother and as a human in general, it may be challenging, and you can feel kind of embarrassed to ask for assistance from other people, but doing so is of the utmost importance when you are coping with postpartum depression or the pressure that comes with being a new mom. You may be less likely to disclose or open up to someone about your symptoms of depression due to cultural and socioeconomic reasons; thus, health care professionals will ask you to inquire about these symptoms both in the antenatal and postpartum period.

If you have just given birth, you might feel too ashamed or guilty to admit to anybody else how difficult their situation is and the difficulties you are facing. However, everybody who has given birth is at risk for developing postpartum depression. Therefore, it is essential to keep in mind that it is not an indication of vulnerability, nor does it serve as proof that you have poor parenting skills.

Advantages of Counseling

- It offers a secure channel for airing your concerns about current events.
    - By providing a secure setting in which to talk things out, counseling can help

you if you are struggling with your mental health, relationships, or circumstances around you. There is a need to speak your mind, but you may hesitate to do so either because of the potential consequences or because you are nervous about what others will think of you. When you suppress unpleasant feelings and thoughts for an extended period, releasing those emotions and ideas is simply a question of time. Therefore, counseling provides you with a space to let out your frustrations and disappointments and let go of grudges and hidden trauma that you have experienced throughout your life which is standing in the way between you and your happiness.

- During your counseling sessions, the therapist protects your confidentiality, so you don't need to worry about other people knowing what you are going through. A conversation with a therapist is not the same as confiding in a loved one or close friend, with whom there is always the possibility of being judged.

- It is the responsibility of a therapist to pay attention to your concerns, inquire about your life, and offer guidance in order to enhance the standard of living you have. During counseling, the therapist will concentrate entirely on you and your needs. An ear that is dedicated to listening to you.

- Counseling will help you improve how you handle and express your feelings.

    o Counseling will assist you in recognizing, expressing, and better regulating your emotions. This is true whether you are struggling with feelings of despair, worry, tension, or rage. You may learn to express and manage your emotions in a healthy way by being more aware of the triggers that cause them, gaining knowledge of the adaptive and maladaptive ways that others deal with similar situations, and modeling how other people do it. You'll be able to avoid the buildup of bad feelings and the undesirable actions that may result from it this way.

- Counseling will teach you how to cope with stress.

    o Being a brand-new mother may be a very trying experience at times. There are a lot of obstacles to overcome in the first year of becoming a parent, such as learning how to nurse your child or going back to work, and postpartum depression just makes the situation worse.

    o Understanding how to handle stress is crucial by identifying the things that might set off stressful circumstances and developing coping strategies that will help you get through those situations. These techniques will be of immeasurable benefit to you in your current situation. In addition, it's probable that you will continue to find a use for the skills and techniques even after your therapy sessions have concluded.

- It will encourage you to take care of yourself.

  - o It is not uncommon for you to have the perception that your child's needs are the focal point of your life; consequently, it might be challenging for you to express the need for personal assistance. You may feel guilty when you admit you require assistance, especially in current times when society asserts that a mother should flourish in her role. This is where the therapist comes in and assists you in overcoming feelings of guilt and assists you in understanding that practicing self-care is important and it's not being selfish. You also look after your newborn and family when you look after yourself.

- It will help you discover your life's purpose.

  - o If you are going through an emotional problem or nothing is making sense anymore, you will typically go through a period in which you temporarily lose your sense of self or identity.

Counseling will assist you in rediscovering your life's purpose, passion, and meaning by guiding you through an investigation of your values and principles, ideas, passions, and memories. This will improve how you feel, and improving how you feel, it will make you a better caregiver to your baby.

- It leads to a higher level of self-acceptance.

  - During motherhood or before, you may have felt insecure about some aspect of how you look, parenting skills, talents, achievements, or personality traits. When you fixate on the bad parts, it might make it difficult for you to see the wonderful qualities that you possess. Counseling can help you learn to embrace your faults and defects as natural components of the human condition. Self-acceptance is the first step in developing feelings of love, compassion for oneself, and a greater sense of self-confidence. By building upon your existing abilities, you will be able to improve the areas in which you now struggle.

- Counseling will help you increase your ability to communicate with others.

  - Going to therapy can be helpful for you as a mom will improve your ability to communicate with your little one. You'll be able to identify stressful situations or anxious emotions and then approach individuals around you for assistance if you work with the correct therapist. Your connection with your companion, your family, and your little one will all benefit from this in the long run.

- It teaches valuable skills.

  - Counseling may teach you endless skills that are helpful in day-to-day life and applicable to a wide variety of situations. These include the ability to communicate effectively and work well with others, as well as problem-solving and strategies for resolving conflicts. Counseling offers a risk-free setting to acquire, hone, and practice these abilities before using them in real-world scenarios outside of the counseling sessions. These things, in the end, contribute to improved physical, mental, and spiritual well-being as a whole.

- Counseling provides room for introspection and personal growth

  - Visiting a counselor allows you to learn about yourself and develop a deeper insight into your character, the things that are important to you, and the ideas you hold. It gives you the opportunity to develop your self-awareness as well as your insight into the part that you play in any difficulties that you may be encountering, and awareness is the first step toward effecting change. It inspires you to go on a personal path toward personal development and motivates you to do so.

- It offers assistance as well as validation.

    o In order for clients to feel at ease disclosing personal information, counselors attempt to create an atmosphere that is secure, welcoming, free of judgment, and full of compassion for them. Compassionate understanding, unwavering positive esteem, and authenticity are considered the three most important qualities in a counselor by the vast majority of clients. Because of this, it is a place in which you do not need to be concerned about being criticized, mocked, or put down in any way. You will have your feelings acknowledged, your circumstances normalized, and you will be reassured that you are not alone in what you are going through.

- It can help treat other medical conditions.

    o In many cases, the symptoms of postpartum depression extend farther than simply and can actually provoke physical problems like cramps, headaches, and insomnia, just to mention a few. A treatment plan tailored to your requirements will be established after you and your therapist have a conversation about your mental and physical health. Therapy plus will eventually improve your physical symptoms.

- Counseling can reduce medical bills.

    o The mind and body are one, I am sure you have heard of this somewhere, and it is true. There is a relationship between your physical and mental well-being. When you receive treatment for an underlying mental health disorder or therapy to assist in regulating emotions and improving mood, this frequently helps improve your physical health as well. There by cutting down costs on your bill and reducing time spent in the hospital.

Tips to Take Care of Your Mental Health After the Baby

One of the most joyful experiences that life has to give is the addition of a new baby to your household, at the same time, it may also be the most stressful experience that life has to offer. After giving birth, the "baby blues" affect a significant number of new mothers, and approximately one in every ten mothers may have postpartum depression.

The first few weeks with a new infant may make you feel completely overwhelmed. Your infant won't have any concept of day or night, and you probably won't get much sleep. There will be many wonderful moments to share with your newborn; nevertheless, even the least difficult babies can be tiresome and unpleasant at times, you will also be learning how to breastfeed if you choose to breastfeed. In addition, you will still be healing from the birth process.

It is possible that even the most insignificant things will set you off at this trying period. Take a moment to relax because this is something that happens to every new mother. When caring for a newborn, it is easy to neglect yourself, but remember it is important to make an effort to take care of yourself as well.

The following are some suggestions on how to take care of your mental health.

- Treat yourself with kindness.

    o Try not to judge yourself based on how you view other parents to be perfect, and you can't come close. Even the other parents you are adoring have their own challenges which you do not know of. A significant portion of what you observe is not accurate, those Instagram images you see are not picture-perfect. Focus on yourself and move at your pace, getting used to the new adjustments, it's easier like that.

- Bring your expectations down to reality.

- You may want to rethink your priorities if you are a parent with high expectations of yourself, like continuing your studies right after giving birth, spotless home, and following a perfect routine. The arrival of a new child has a way of upending established patterns and destroying any sense of predictability. They tend to be unpredictable even when you think you now know their daily routine. When you have a new baby, one of the most important skills you can learn is how to let go of high expectations.

- Allow yourself to care in a way that you can.

  - The greatest method to care for your child is the approach that works best for you, so give yourself permission to do it that way. Everyone has something to say about parenting, but the most important thing for you as a new mom to do is to figure out what works best for you. It's possible that you won't find the optimal approach until you put in some practice. Keep doing what's successful for you, and stop worrying about what other people think.

- Seek social assistance.

  - It's possible that confiding in a close friend or member of your family can help you feel better. There are other individuals and places you may turn to for help if you do not feel comfortable discussing your emotions with those you know personally. If you are not comfortable with opening up to people you might know. You might as well take advantage of technology by having phone therapy, joining online support groups, etc. Do not feel lonely because there are a lot of people that are more than willing to be there for you, from family members to friends. Having meaningful social connections is especially crucial in the postpartum period.

- Get enough sleep.

  o It's common knowledge that newborns are renowned for keeping parents up at night, and you might actually start believing that's their job. Failure to sleep may amplify emotional responses and unpleasant sensations. Find a reliable friend, family, or babysitter who can look after your child while you close your eyes.

  o During these first few weeks, it is likely that your newborn baby may not sleeping all the way through the night. You could find that getting some rest by napping or going to bed earlier helps. You can try to sleep when your baby sleeps, or you can ask for turns in the hours of the day or night to swap watch over baby duties with your partner.

Alternatively, you can ask a trusted sibling or friend to watch over your baby as you try to sleep for a few hours. Even if they won't be consecutive, at least you'll have received enough rest to be able to operate reasonably well. The more you can sleep, the more you can relax, and this will improve your mood and the care you give your baby. It is advised that you keep up with this preservation of your sleep demands for at least a month after giving birth. If you are willing to, you can hire a trusted professional to help out with all duties while you rest.

- Eat well and exercise regularly.

  o Eating healthily is not enough to treat PPD on its own. Nevertheless, making healthier eating habits a regular part of your routine may help you feel better overall and provide your body with the nutrition it requires. You should try meal planning and include healthy snacks when you want to snack.

- Get moving.

  o Soft exercises are another thing that will complement a healthy diet to improve your health during and after the postpartum period. Relax as you work-out. Do not try to rush yourself by trying to do strenuous exercises. There is no need to lift heavy weights or run tens of kilometers on the treadmill. After you feel you have recovered, you can ask for clearance from your healthcare professional, and you can try to start with some light weights at the gym or at home.

- Avoid isolating yourself.

  o It's possible that as days and nights pass by as a new mom, you might start feeling all alone. It is a known fact by now that sharing your thoughts and emotions with others might positively affect your mood. If you are a new mom, you might find it beneficial to routinely speak with other moms who have passed the stage you are at and how they cope with motherhood. If you are suffering from postpartum depression (PPD), talking to those experienced moms will help lower levels of depression compared to new mothers who do not regularly communicate with experienced mothers. There is no denying the value of social connection. Make every effort to leave the house or, at the very least, engage in supportive conversation with other adults and moms, physically or on the phone.

- Consider breastfeeding.

  o Mothers who breastfeed have a lower chance of experiencing PPD. It's possible that this alleged protection will last all the way until the sixth month following birth. You can breastfeed if you take pleasure in doing so. It is important to know that there are some instances where women who breastfeed can also experience depression.

- Get lost in music.

  - Music evokes feelings in you, makes you reminisce, and it has the potential to take you back to your roots. It has an effect on brain function. Make a playlist of music that makes you happy and allows you to experience your emotions to help you get by the day. It is therapeutic.

- Don't forget the benefit in the long run.

  - When you have a brand-new baby, a single day might feel like a lifetime, yet it can also make you think time is moving too fast. Remember that this is only a season, even on those occasions when it seems to drag on forever and everything seems to be going wrong. It shall come to pass, and you will have more time to yourself as your baby gains full independence.

Chapter 8

Preparing for Changing Family Dynamics

Pregnancy and Work

It can be difficult to maintain balance at work and in your personal life when you are pregnant. However, you can set yourself up for success with proper time management practices and a little honesty.

- Mind your medication.

  - In the midst of the stress of your workday, do not forget to take your prenatal vitamins and iron supplements. You should not ignore your iron tablets because the results can be bad in no time. You could start feeling dizzy and lose concentration on the outside, but when we dig deeper, we realize you were sabotaging your body and your baby's health by skipping medication. Your growing baby requires blood, so you need to supplement in order to meet the increasing demand. Avoid putting your baby's development at risk just so you receive praise for expertly managing a project and advancing your professional standing.

- Notify your superiors about the pregnancy.

    o You may want to let your supervisor know as soon as possible about your baby being on the way. This is of utmost significance if you need to take time off from work to attend several checkups and appointments with the doctor. There are times when you will feel overly tired and cannot fulfill your usual duties, and other times, the job requires you to put in a little more effort than you usually do. In such situations, you will want to make sure that some of your responsibilities are shifted to avoid falling behind or being micromanaged. Telling your superiors about your pregnancy also helps them establish appropriate expectations regarding the work you will be doing at this period of your life.

- Be sincere regarding your emotions.

    o Stay honest with yourself and acknowledge it when you are not feeling well or when you can no longer reach your full potential. This helps you determine what responsibilities you need help with, and it also assists you when telling your superiors and your coworkers about the pregnancy. As your pregnancy progresses, you experience weight gain and become exhausted. You may even find it a little challenging to move around, which may cause problems at home and work. Your coworkers will appreciate your honesty, and it's probable that they will pitch in to help make up for the lost time. Remember to show your appreciation by putting in extra effort on the days that you feel like you have more energy.

- Share the news with your colleagues.

    o Letting your coworkers know about your pregnancy makes it easier for you to maintain a balance between your work and the pregnancy. When you are not feeling well and fall behind, your coworkers don't assume you are being careless when they know it's because of the pregnancy. Besides, if you do not communicate your troubles with them, they cannot help you. When working with other people you are not very comfortable with, you can simply let them know you are exhausted.

- Establish good eating habits.

    o You need to maintain a healthy diet throughout your pregnancy to reduce the severity of many issues that might arise. Eating well will also prevent you from putting on excessive weight, which would contribute to a less active lifestyle after birth.

- Exercise regularly.

    o Even if your schedule is tight and you only have a few minutes to break, direct some of that time toward exercise. Staying active keeps your blood flowing and lifts your mood, which aids in nourishing your developing baby. You can even sign up for a workout class for pregnant women. Joining a workout group also gives you an opportunity to know other women who are expecting babies and stay motivated.

Knowing When to Stop

It is up to you to decide when you should slow down or completely stop working while you are pregnant. While some expecting mothers continue their regular activities without problematic symptoms right up to labor, pregnancy complications force others to stop working early during the process. Some women strive to reserve their maternity leave for after their baby arrives so they can have more time to bond without the pressure of having to leave for work.

Making the choice to slow down or stop working isn't something that comes easily for everyone. That is because we all have a lot of things that go into our decision-making process, including issues such as bills, quality of living, health, and the benefits of taking time off. If your living situation requires you to work, you may find it difficult or even impossible to stop working. Those whose living arrangements are more flexible afford a short break every once in a while. That is because we all have a lot of things that go into our decision-making process, including issues such as bills, quality of living, health, and the benefits of taking time off. If your living situation requires you to work, you may find it difficult or even impossible to stop working. Those whose living arrangements are more flexible afford a short break every once in a while.

If you do not encounter any complications with your pregnancy, you may be able to continue working your regular job until you are close to labor. Although you are recommended to stay active during pregnancy and doing most of the chores around the house is safe, you may want to avoid household activities that require standing for long hours, lifting heavy weights, or putting too much strain on your body. Additionally, it is best to avoid physically demanding chores if you encounter any medical reasons to stop working. It may be time for you to slow down or put your work life on pause if you are living in any of the situations below.

- Your work environment is dangerous.
    - o It is in your best interest to inform your employer about your pregnancy if there is any possibility you or the baby could

get hurt due to a hazardous workplace. Work environments that subject you to excessive noise, radiation, and chemicals may harm your developing baby. In certain circumstances, it may not be a challenge to avoid all dangers when doing your duties at work. It is best to request that your boss either change your required workload or give you an alternative that does not. It is one that puts your baby's life in danger. If your boss won't help you with a suitable job during pregnancy, you may want to stop working before your baby's wellness pays the price.

- You experience preterm complications.

  - No one wants to go into labor too soon. We mostly fear for our little ones, wondering if they would be okay if they arrived before they were ready. If you are experiencing symptoms of preterm issues, it is essential to engage your doctor and discuss if you should take a break from work during pregnancy. Some of the warning indicators of preterm problems are as follows:

    - vaginal bleeding

    - contractions

    - abdominal cramping

    - backache

    - leaking vaginal fluid

When your body begins getting ready for labor and you start experiencing some of these situations, it is best to avoid working too much or stop altogether.

- You can no longer meet expectations.

    o Routine desk jobs can become tedious too! Even if your job does not require a lot of physical labor, you can experience emotional pressure that leads to worry and stress. At some point during your pregnancy, sitting the whole day can be difficult, leading to swelling in the legs and adding a further strain to your abdomen. Another indicator to stop working during this period is if you feel that your job is becoming more demanding or you realize that you can no longer concentrate on it adequately.

- You have a high-risk pregnancy.

    o Be on the lookout for symptoms and signs that could indicate a high-risk pregnancy so you can take better care of yourself at work or stop if necessary. A number of factors can contribute to a woman having a high-risk pregnancy, and some are:

        - multiple pregnancies

        - alcohol consumption

        - unhealthy levels of blood pressure

        - poor development of the fetus

- smoking

- pre-eclampsia in past pregnancies

- heart or blood disorders

- diabetes

Working while experiencing pregnancy difficulties makes your situation even more challenging. While some women find themselves unable to walk or get up due to pregnancy complications, others struggle on their feet, depending on the severity of their situation. Whichever the case, it is preferable to call it quits when you realize that you need to tread more carefully during your pregnancy.

Making Time for Your Partner

After having a baby, it takes significant time and effort to keep the relationship with your partner strong. What's worse, your little one demands the same two things from you—energy and time. The responsibility of looking after your tiny human is so demanding and time-consuming that you might not get to breathe even in your spare time. Spending self-care activities can feel like an excessive luxury during this time. You will find time to discuss who buys diapers and who pays rent, but you get fewer opportunities to bond as compared to before you had the baby. If you do not do something to spend more quality time with your partner, your relationship can slip through your fingers before you know it.

You may encounter a number of issues in your relationship, especially if you live with your partner, married or not. Apart from failing to make time for each other, everyday visitors who want to see the baby and doing the laundry and dishes, you may realize there is so much to quarrel about. Housework after having a baby can feel as though you have never had such a large number of tasks that need to be completed in a limited time. As a result, you may get the impression that your person isn't doing their fair share of the work, even when they try by all means to squeeze out a break for you.

You cannot force yourself to help around the house when your body feels otherwise. This is especially true when you have just given birth and still need to heal. Regardless of the stage you are at, the least you can do for your caring partner is make time for them.

Below are tips to let your loved one know you appreciate them.

- Be there even when you can't be.
  - You are most likely to tire easily after bringing that mini you home. You may realize you need to spend a lot of time sleeping both during the day and at night. If your partner goes to work and returns at night, they might not want to disturb your sleep in the morning when they leave or at night when they return. That is because they understand that you need as much rest as you can get during this time. It's not your fault the baby wakes you up during early hours and keeps you busy during the day, but it is not your partner's either! You can still let them know you care by leaving them small hints that show you think of them. Try leaving them small notes with heartwarming messages, then transition to something grander such as preparing their favorite meal and waiting up for them—it's just one night!
  - Even during the day, it is not necessary to wait for sunset just so you can have a romantic conversation with your partner. You can develop post-work routines for your loved one's off days. If their off days are not enough time, pick a day once every two weeks, every month, or even every week to meet

them halfway or pick them up from work.

- Respect your couple-time.

    o Try establishing a consistent bedtime for your baby to simplify your couple time. With your baby sleeping, you and your partner can relax and enjoy being together while doing something as simple as watching a movie or cooking together. Avoid making excuses during the weekend. Grab your backpack, the pram, and the diaper bag, and head out to have fun as a couple-plus-one to participate in a fun activity. There are plenty of baby-friendly destinations that will allow you to relax with your partner once the tiny human falls asleep, but if you don't want to be in public or go anywhere, you can still make a date night at home. once your little one has calmed down for the night. It does not have to be the whole night, but at least for a few hours, and do anything you want to do.

    o 'Anything' does not mean you should slouch off to finish your household chores or return calls that you couldn't return earlier-respect a couple of times! You can spend some time sitting together even if only for a minute. Simply setting aside time for each other can help you feel closer to one another.

- Don't be boring!

  - Make an effort to have a proper dating night rather than taking it home all the time. You can make arrangements for a babysitter, think about switching babysitting duties with other mothers, or consider asking a close friend or family member to watch your little one for a few hours. Remember, it is not necessary for the date night to be a full night; you just want to spend quality time with one another.

Conclusion

Your *someone* bids you farewell and hopes you have learned vital information about first-time pregnancy, childbirth, and postpartum.

In this book, we have covered pregnancy basics, from conception to the development of unborn babies. We have also looked into the changes that take place in our bodies during the three stages of pregnancy, from hormonal changes occurring on a biological level to emotional and physical changes resulting from hormonal fluctuations. In light of how challenging the time after delivery can be, we have also dissected postpartum depression and discussed life after the baby comes.

If you enjoyed this read and found it informative, feel free to share the knowledge with your family and friends.

Glossary

Acupuncturist: a trained professional who has expertise in an ancient Chinese medical practice that involves the insertion of tiny needles at specific points of the body for treatment purposes

Amniocentesis: a medical procedure that involves tapping amniotic fluid for genetic or chromosomal diagnosis

Anaesthesiologist: a medical practitioner specialized in giving medications that reduce or eliminate pain.

Antenatal: the period during pregnancy that involves routine medical checkups and consultation

Blastocyst: a rapidly dividing ball of cells that forms after Day 5 of fertilization of the female egg and later develops into an embryo

Braxton Hicks contractions: irregular, non-sustained abdominal contractions that indicate false labor

Chiropractic care: a complementary healthcare service that deals with diagnosis and treatment of problems that affect joints, bones, muscles, and the spine

Chorionic villus sampling: a medical procedure that involves taking a tissue sample from the placenta for genetic anomalies diagnostic purposes

CPR (cardiopulmonary resuscitation): a medical procedure used in emergencies to help improve blood circulation. It is also applied when the heart stops beating or when someone drowns.

Cystic fibrosis: a genetic medical condition that causes a build-up of sticky mucus in the lungs and other organs

Embryonic period: this period starts after implantation and ends in Week 8, after which an embryo becomes a fetus

Estrogen: a hormone that helps develop female sexual traits, and assists in the growth and development of a fetus during pregnancy

Germinal stage: this is the first stage in human development, it starts after the egg has been fertilized till it's been implanted in the uterus

Gravidarum emesis: vomiting during pregnancy

Human chorionic gonadotropin: a hormone that is produced during pregnancy to help maintain the pregnancy and integrity of the uterus

Hypnosis: a state in which one's awareness is reduced, like sleep mode

Implantation: when a fertilized egg infiltrates and attaches to the uterus to facilitate its growth

Lactational amenorrhea: a natural contraceptive method that can be used if a woman is exclusively breastfeeding for up six months from childbirth

Meconium: green, dark-like stool that is a baby's first fecal excretion

Postpartum: the period after giving birth to 6 weeks during which the uterus starts recovering and hormones go back to normal

Pre-eclampsia: a medical condition that occurs after the 20th week of pregnancy, and is characterized by elevated blood pressure levels and protein in urine

Pregnancy associated plasma protein-A: a protein that aids placenta growth and implantation

Progesterone: a hormone that helps regulate the menstrual cycle, and helps the body not to expel the fetus during pregnancy

Prognosis: a likely to turn out of a condition

Psychotherapy: a form of treatment that involves counseling or talk therapy for mental health management

Rhesus factor: a blood grouping system that is determined by the protein present on the surface of the red blood cells.

Serotonin: is a hormone that helps regulate mood and cognitive functions

SSRIs: selective serotonin reuptake inhibitors are a class of antidepressants drugs used to treat depression

Zygote: a fertilized egg that is formed by the union of a sperm and egg

References

ACOG committee opinion no. 764. (2019). *Obstetrics & Gynecology,* *133*(2), e151–e155. https://doi.org/10.1097/aog.0000000000003083

American College of Obstetricians and Gynecologists. (2017, May). *Medications for pain relief during labor and delivery.* ACOG. https://www.acog.org/womens-health/faqs/medications-for-pain-relief-during-labor-and-delivery

Cherry, K. (2020, June 1). *How a baby develops during the prenatal period.* Verywell Mind. https://www.verywellmind.com/stages-of-prenatal-development-2795073

Deepak, D., Kumari, A., Mohanty, R., Prakash, J., Kumar, T., & Priye, S. (2022). Effects of epidural analgesia on labor pain and course of labor in primigravid parturients: A prospective non-randomized comparative study. *Cureus,* *14*(6). https://doi.org/10.7759/cureus.26090

DelRosario, G., Chang, C., & Lee, E. (2013). February 2013 - volume 26 - issue 2 : *Journal of the american academy of pas.* JAAPA. https://journals.lww.com/jaapa/Fulltext/2013/02000/Postpartum_depression__Symptoms

Hutchison, J., Mahdy, H., & Hutchison, J. (2019, November 16). *Stages of labor.* Nih; StatPearls Publishing. https://www.ncbi.nlm.nih.gov/books/NBK54 4290/

Kim, H. I., Choo, S. P., Han, S. W., & Kim, E. H. (2019). Benefits and risks of induction of labor at 39 or more weeks in uncomplicated nulliparous women: A retrospective, observational study. *Obstetrics & Gynecology Science, 62*(1), 19. https://doi.org/10.5468/ogs.2019.62.1.19

Leduc, D., Biringer, A., Lee, L., Dy, J., Corbett, T., Leduc, D., Biringer, A., Duperron, L., Dy, J., Lange, I., Lee, L., Muise, S., Parish, B., Regush, L., Wilson, K., Yeung, G., Crane, J., Gagnon, R., Sawchuck, D., & Senikas, V. (2013). Induction of Labour. *Journal of Obstetrics and Gynaecology Canada, 35*(9), 840–857. https://doi.org/10.1016/s1701-2163(15)30842-2

Stiles, J., & Jernigan, T. L. (2010). The basics of brain development. *Neuropsychology Review, 20*(4), 327–348. https://doi.org/10.1007/s11065-010-9148-4

Weiss, R. E. (n.d.). *Coping tips for each stage of labor.* Verywell Family. https://www.verywellfamily.com/online-childbirth-education-class-three-2758530

Image References

Amaya, C. (2019, May 7). *White and blue textiles.* Pexels. https://images.pexels.com/photos/2252000/p exels-photo-2252000.jpeg?cs=srgb&dl=pexels-chloe-amaya-2252000.jpg&fm=jpg

Borba, J. (2019, November 24). *Newborn baby breastfeeding.* Pexels. https://images.pexels.com/photos/3279208/p exels-photo-3279208.jpeg?cs=srgb&dl=pexels-jonathan-borba-3279208.jpg&fm=jpg

Chagas, M. (2019, February 8). *Woman wearing white shirt near white printer paper.* Pexels. https://images.pexels.com/photos/1876279/p exels-photo-1876279.jpeg?cs=srgb&dl=pexels-marcelo-chagas-1876279.jpg&fm=jpg

Cup of Couple. (2021, April 7). *Food in a bowl on brown surface.* Pexels. https://images.pexels.com/photos/7660435/p exels-photo-7660435.jpeg?cs=srgb&dl=pexels-cup-of-couple-7660435.jpg&fm=jpg

Fortunato, W. (2021, January 4). *Professional massage therapist doing massage for cute little black girl.* Pexels. https://images.pexels.com/photos/6393191/p exels-photo-6393191.jpeg?cs=srgb&dl=pexels-william-fortunato-6393191.jpg&fm=jpg

Grabowska, C. (2020, May 18). *Blood samples.* Pexels. https://images.pexels.com/photos/4047146/p

exels-photo-4047146.jpeg?cs=srgb&dl=pexels-
karolina-grabowska-4047146.jpg&fm=jpg

Grabowska, K. (2020, December 3). *Woman in white long
sleeves lying on sofa.* Pexels.
https://images.pexels.com/photos/6255631/p
exels-photo-6255631.jpeg?cs=srgb&dl=pexels-
karolina-grabowska-6255631.jpg&fm=jpg

Kamau, G. (2019, August 13). *Pregnant woman lying on
green grass fields.* Pexels.
https://images.pexels.com/photos/2781219/p
exels-photo-2781219.jpeg?cs=srgb&dl=pexels-
george-jr-kamau-2781219.jpg&fm=jpg

Kelley, L. (2017, March 7). *Two person laying on white mat.*
Pexels.
https://images.pexels.com/photos/341520/pe
xels-photo-341520.jpeg?cs=srgb&dl=pexels-
leah-kelley-341520.jpg&fm=jpg

Mart Production. (2021, March 10). *Birthplan.* Pexels.
https://images.pexels.com/photos/7088526/p
exels-photo-7088526.jpeg?cs=srgb&dl=pexels-
mart-production-7088526.jpg&fm=jpg

Mart Production. (2021, March 10). *Photo of ob-gyn doing
a test.* Pexels.
https://images.pexels.com/photos/7088841/p
exels-photo-7088841.jpeg?cs=srgb&dl=pexels-
mart-production-7088841.jpg&fm=jpg

Piacquadio, A. (2018, March 23). *Woman sleeping on white
bed holding blue pillow.* Pexels.
https://images.pexels.com/photos/935742/pe

xels-photo-935742.jpeg?cs=srgb&dl=pexels-andrea-piacquadio-935742.jpg&fm=jpg

Resch, A. (2021, June 4). *High angle shot of a cute infant taking a bath.* Pexels. https://images.pexels.com/photos/8203562/pexels-photo-8203562.jpeg?cs=srgb&dl=pexels-andreas-resch-8203562.jpg&fm=jpg

Ribeiro, B. (2021, October 6). *Doctor holding newborn baby.* Pexels. https://images.pexels.com/photos/9747426/pexels-photo-9747426.jpeg?cs=srgb&dl=pexels-barbara-ribeiro-9747426.jpg&fm=jpg

Rodnae Productions. (2020, December 10). *White flower beside brown box with pregnancy test.* Pexels. https://images.pexels.com/photos/6148907/pexels-photo-6148907.jpeg?cs=srgb&dl=pexels-rodnae-productions-6148907.jpg&fm=jpg

Sayduang, P. (2020, September 22). *Top view of syringe with pills.* Pexels. https://images.pexels.com/photos/4541337/pexels-photo-4541337.jpeg?cs=srgb&dl=pexels-piyapong-sayduang-4541337.jpg&fm=jpg

Shevtsova, D. (2020, June 2). *Photo of female hand holding a bowl of green vegetables.* Pexels. https://images.pexels.com/photos/4117550/pexels-photo-4117550.jpeg?cs=srgb&dl=pexels-daria-shevtsova-4117550.jpg&fm=jpg

Shkraba, A. (2021, April 16). *Pregnant woman meditating at home.* Pexels.

https://images.pexels.com/photos/7524702/p
exels-photo-7524702.jpeg?cs=srgb&dl=pexels-
antoni-shkraba-7524702.jpg&fm=jpg

Shvets, A. (2022, March 4). *Mother giving baby a bottle of milk.* Pexels. https://images.pexels.com/photos/11369278/
pexels-photo-
11369278.jpeg?cs=srgb&dl=pexels-anna-
shvets-11369278.jpg&fm=jpg

Vdnhieu. (2021, March 1). *Depression.* Pixabay.
https://cdn.pixabay.com/photo/2021/03/01/
14/40/girl-6059889_960_720.jpg